IN THE NATIONAL GALLERY OF CANADA

"One of the most beautiful chapels in the land"

IN THE NATIONAL GALLERY OF CANADA

"One of the most beautiful chapels in the land"

LUC NOPPEN

NATIONAL GALLERY OF CANADA
OTTAWA 1988

**Canadian Cataloguing in
Publication Data**
National Gallery of Canada.
One of the most beautiful chapels
in the land.

Issued also in French under the title:
Une des plus belles chapelles du pays.

ISBN 0–88884–576–6

1. Rideau Chapel.
2. Chapels–Ontario–Ottawa.
3. Bouillon, Georges, 1841–1932.

I. Noppen, Luc, 1949–   II. Title.

NA5247 .087 N38 1988   726.7
C88–099509–2

Design: Eiko Emori Inc.

PRINTED IN CANADA

Cover
South aisle of the restored and
reassembled chapel of the Rideau
Street Convent, Ottawa, as installed in
the National Gallery of Canada. Detail
of Plate VIII, photograph by Malak,
May 1988.

Photo Credits
Cover, plates III–VIII Malak, Ottawa,
for the National Gallery of Canada;
plate I Commonwealth Historic
Resource Management Limited,
Ottawa; plate II National Research
Council, Ottawa; figs 1, 38, 47 Na-
tional Capital Commission, Ottawa;
fig. 2 Jean-Marie Versteege/National
Archives of Canada (PA 167025);
fig. 3 Rusins Kaufmanis for *The Ottawa
Citizen;* fig. 4 Jean-Marie Versteege/
National Archives of Canada
(PA 167024); fig. 5 Jean-Marie
Versteege/National Archives of
Canada (PA 167018); figs 6, 7 Peter
Kellner/National Capital Commission;
fig. 8 The Canadian Press, Toronto;
figs 9, 20, 21, 26, 28 Algonquin
College, Architectural Technology,
Ottawa; figs 10, 11 National Research
Council, Ottawa; figs 12, 13, 59 Na-
tional Gallery of Canada, Ottawa;
figs 14, 15 Éditeur officiel du Québec;
fig. 16 National Archives of Canada
(PA 33908); fig. 17 National Archives
of Canada (C 3347); figs 18, 44, 45,
48 Archives of the Sisters of Charity,
Ottawa; fig. 19 National Archives of
Canada (PA 31172); fig. 22 W. J.
Topley/National Archives of Canada
(PA 8671); fig. 23 Hans Wild in James
Pope-Hennessy, *The Houses of Parlia-
ment* (London: B.T. Batsford Ltd.,
1953), p.50/copy photo provided by
the author; figs 24, 25, 27, 49, 58,
66 provided by the author; fig. 29
National Archives of Canada
(PA 8768); figs 30, 60 Gatineau,
Church of Saint-François-de-Sales, par-
ish archives; figs 31, 33, 56, 57, 64
Sylvie Tanguay, Quebec City; fig. 32
William Notman/National Archives
of Canada (PA 117428); fig. 34 Na-
tional Archives of Canada (C 2463);
figs 35, 69–72 Archives nationales du
Québec in Trois-Rivières; fig. 36 Trois-
Pistoles, parish archives; figs 37, 53,
61 Archives of the archdiocese of
Ottawa; figs 39, 42, 46 City of Ottawa
Archives; fig. 40 W.J. Topley/copy
photo, National Gallery of Canada;
fig. 41 National Archives of Canada
(PA 27087); fig. 43 National Archives
of Canada; figs 50, 51, 52 M.E. Burns/
National Capital Commission, Ottawa;
fig. 54 Archives of the diocese of
Rimouski; fig. 55 National Archives
of Canada (PA 12457); fig. 62 Louis
Bélanger/National Archives of Canada
(PA 138834); fig. 63 Province de
Québec/Inventaire des œuvres d'art;
fig. 65 National Archives of Canada
(PA 23742); fig. 67 Bic, parish
archives; fig. 68 National Archives
of Canada (C 10175); fig. 73 Musée
du Québec.

CONTENTS

ACKNOWLEDGEMENTS

The author expresses his appreciation to all those who have contributed to this project, and in particular to Charles C. Hill, curator of Canadian art at the National Gallery of Canada, who conceived the idea for this book and guided it through to realization; Sylvie Tanguay, research assistant; Hélène Ziarko, editor; Claude Thibault of the Musée du Québec; Sister Marcelle Gratton, archivist of the archdiocese of Ottawa; Canon Léo Bérubé, archivist of the diocese of Rimouski; Claire Hemelin-Rossignol; and Clara Marceau. Special thanks also go to the publications staff of the National Gallery of Canada, under the direction of Serge Thériault, who were responsible for preparing the manuscript for publication: editors Verena Ossent and Norman Dahl, and photo editor Colleen Evans.

FOREWORD

Architecture is intended to fulfill certain functions within a particular built and natural landscape. Architecture should be understood in this context, even though its surroundings may have changed radically. To dismantle a building and reconstruct it within a totally different environment only provides us with part of the information and should be undertaken only in an extreme situation.

Such was the case with the chapel of the Convent of Our Lady of the Sacred Heart, Ottawa, better known as the Rideau Street Convent. Sold by the Sisters of Charity, because of declining enrolment and deteriorating physical plant, the convent, of which the chapel was only one part, was threatened with total destruction. Concerned citizens – including the late Hazen Sise, R.A.J. Phillips, and Humphrey Carver of A Capital for Canadians, Mary Roaf of Action Sandy Hill, and Barry Padolsky of the Save the Convent committee – led a public campaign to ensure the survival of this outstanding example of nineteenth-century neo-Gothic architecture. Though in the end nothing could stop the demolition of the convent, their efforts were not in vain. Through the active intervention of the National Capital Commission and with the assistance of the Department of Indian Affairs and Northern Development and the National Research Council, the chapel interior was dismantled, acquired for the National Gallery, and preserved for future generations.

If the survival of the chapel was the result of community effort and the commitment of the Gallery's director, Jean Sutherland Boggs, and the curator of early Canadian art, Jean Trudel, its reconstruction has also been possible through the efforts of many individuals and government departments. When in 1984 the Gallery, with the encouragement of its director, Joseph Martin, decided to restore the chapel interior, the Canadian Parks Service of Environment Canada offered the assistance of Julian Smith, to determine the approach and guidelines for the restoration, as well as the services of the restoration architect Ken Elder, who has directed this aspect of the project to its completion with the assistance of Anna Kozlowski. Engineering advice was provided by Claude Lévesque, also of the Parks Service. Harold Kalman, of Commonwealth Historic Resource Management Limited, engaged by the Gallery for the inventory, restoration, and installation of the surviving elements, has been a keen supporter of this project. Additional assistance has been provided by the Canadian Conservation Institute, the Historic Resource Conservation Branch of the Parks Service, the National Capital Commission, and Canada Museums Construction Corporation. The measured drawings made in 1971 by Algonquin College students, led by Victor Hughes under the direction of Peter Arends, have proved to be invaluable throughout.

Yet this project would not have been possible without the support of the Friends of the National Gallery. Under the chairmanship of Agnes Benidickson and the energetic direction of Doris Smith, the Chapel Committee of the Friends has pursued a national campaign to raise considerable funds toward the restoration and reconstruction of the chapel. In this the Committee has been ably staffed by numerous volunteers and supported by the Rideau Convent Alumnae Association. The assistance of Sister Sainte-Madeleine and Sister Louise Marguerite of the Sisters of Charity has been greatly appreciated.

The realization of this project has taken four years of hard work, ably coordinated by Geoff Hoare of the Gallery's New Building Office. Deborah Tunis initiated and has maintained a long-term interest in the project and Charles C. Hill, curator of Canadian art, has provided ongoing advice.

I am especially pleased that Luc Noppen has written this scholarly text on the architecture of the Rideau chapel and its architect the Canon Georges Bouillon. Mr. Noppen has ably situated this architectural masterwork within the context of nineteenth-century revivalist movements and within a tradition of ecclesiastical architecture in Canada.

The installation of this chapel interior in the National Gallery of Canada and the publication of this book offer new directions for the Gallery in encouraging an understanding of our architectural heritage. I am certain that a greater appreciation of our architecture will result in increased efforts to preserve it within its original context. Museums have a great responsibility to highlight and define the importance of objects within their walls, but the aesthetic understanding attained by that experience must be realized within our own neighbourhoods, in the streets of our towns and cities, and in the preservation of our environment.

Dr. Shirley L. Thomson
Director

Plate I
This colour lithographed postcard
shows the chapel of the Convent
of Our Lady of the Sacred Heart,
Ottawa, built in 1887–88, as it
appeared about 1900, with a decor
of trompe-l'oeil fans and columns
painted on the flat wall of the apse.
The architect, Georges Bouillon,
like the artists of the Italian Renaissance, used the trompe-l'oeil technique to make the choir seem
larger, an effect further deepened by
the arrangement of the woodwork
and the altars. This first painted
decor disappeared about 1910.
(C.R. McGuire Collection)

Plate II
The chapel of the Convent of Our
Lady of the Sacred Heart in May
1972, a few days before the interior
was dismantled and removed from
the chapel building, slated for
demolition a few days later.

Plate III (previous page)
General view of the architectural decor of the chapel of the Convent of Our Lady of the Sacred Heart, as reconstructed and installed in the National Gallery of Canada. The restoration specialists used as their guide the appearance of the interior when it was dismantled in 1972. A lighter palette was used in 1888 – gold, creamy white, beige, and pale green. The present colours, featuring shades of blue, date from a restoration program in 1944. The cast-iron columns were marbleized to disguise the utilitarian material.

Plate IV
The woodwork of the choir and altars in the chapel of the Rideau Street Convent. Using as his model the great choir screens of Gothic cathedrals, Georges Bouillon developed a structure in wood that would create a semicircular sanctuary in the rectangular space of the chapel. This decor reproduces, in simpler form, the stalls and reredos of the Churches of Notre Dame in Montreal and Ottawa.

Plate V
The chapel, seen from the choir, as reassembled in the National Gallery in 1987–88. The vault is an assembly of modules, worked in wood, and affixed to soffits and embellished with mouldings. The interest of this vault lies more in its overall concept – borrowed from the English Perpendicular style prevalent during the Tudor period – than in the detail of its execution which, in fact, was quite standard for the time.

Plate VI
The stained-glass windows of the chapel, installed in new frames, contribute to the presentation of the reconstructed architectural decor. New stencilling on the plastered walls replicates the decorative scheme of the chapel as it appeared before being dismantled, and ensures that the original architectural elements are integrated into their new surroundings.

Plate VII
The cusped mouldings, the trefoil shapes, the flat contoured arches containing rosettes shaped like four-leaved clovers evince a very personal style of creating ornamental effect. It is a style that Georges Bouillon had already used during construction of the interior decor of the Cathedral of Notre Dame in Ottawa from 1876 to 1883.

Plate VIII
South aisle, looking toward the
organ loft, of the reassembled chapel
of the Rideau Street Convent in
the National Gallery of Canada.

I

THE CHAPEL WITHIN THE MUSEUM

When the new National Gallery of Canada opened in May 1988, an exhibit at the heart of the Canadian Galleries was just marking its centennial. On 25 June 1888, the chapel of the Convent of Our Lady of the Sacred Heart, Ottawa, commonly known as the Rideau Street Convent, was dedicated by Monsignor Joseph-Thomas Duhamel, archbishop of Ottawa. A century later, the chapel began a new life as an architectural work on exhibit in the National Gallery.

The Process of Validation

A museum, by its very nature, endows a work of art with a certain status if only by preserving it for posterity. Thus, the installation of the interior decor of the chapel of the Rideau Street Convent in the National Gallery confers on that work a particular standing, and it is noteworthy, too, in that few museums have chosen to showcase elements of architecture. But this work was a centre of attention long before it entered the Gallery. Its preservation came about as the result of an unprecedented mobilization of community effort; an informed public demanded that it be saved and, in effect, gave the National Gallery a mandate to ensure that it was put to proper use.

In December 1970 the news went out: the city block bounded by Rideau, Waller, Besserer, and Cumberland Streets, on the edge of

Ottawa's historic neighbourhoods of Sandy Hill and Lower Town, had been put up for sale by the Sisters of Charity. The year before, the nuns had withdrawn to the mother house on Bruyère Street, citing the exodus of population from the centre of the city to the suburbs, declining enrolment, shortage of teaching staff, and deteriorating older buildings as their reasons for abandoning the site. First to react was the association known as A Capital for Canadians, "a citizens' group devoted to the National Capital's development as a vital, progressive centre in Canada." On 17 February 1971, members of the group's heritage committee – including Hazen Sise, Humphrey Carver, and Mary Anne Phillips – with R.H. Hubbard of the National Gallery of Canada, toured the convent and were dazzled by the beauty of the chapel, an "undiscovered treasure."[1] Fearing that the sale of the complex would almost certainly mean demolition, the chairman of the group's heritage committee, R.A.J. Phillips, on 9 March wrote to the nuns asking them to consider delaying the sale until suitable buyers could be found who would respect the heritage value of the buildings.[2] Other concerned groups – notably Action Sandy Hill and the ad hoc Save the Convent committee, headed by Mary Roaf and Barry Padolsky – supported the

The sketch map of downtown Ottawa indicates the site of the National Gallery of Canada on Nepean Point (upper left) and the former Rideau Street Convent (far right). The shaded area in the floor plan diagram of the Gallery marks the location of the reconstructed interior of the chapel of the convent.

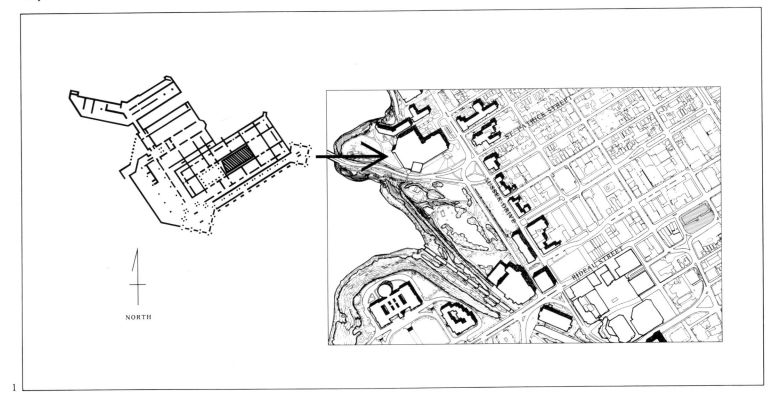

NORTH

1

heritage committee in a campaign to alert the public to the potential danger of losing the convent and to encourage public discussion of the issues.[3] An article in *Le Droit* on 20 March 1971 headed: "Can we remain indifferent to the demolition of this testament to the past?" offered its readers a long history of the building. On the same day, *The Ottawa Journal* also published a story titled "A nostalgic last look at Rideau Street Convent." Both newspapers emphasized the history of the convent and its valuable architectural features – notably the interior of the 1888 chapel, the work of Canon Georges Bouillon, a priest of the diocese of Ottawa. On 26 March, R.A.J. Phillips, in a letter in *The Ottawa Citizen* headlined "Don't wreck it," underscored the importance of the structure: "Architects state that this complex of buildings . . . comprises the largest concentration of pre- and post-Confederation construction in Ottawa. The little-known chapel is strikingly beautiful."[4]

In May 1971 came more news: *The Ottawa Journal* reported that the convent had been sold.[5] Members of A Capital for Canadians immediately met with the buyer, Glenview Realty Corporation, to argue for the building's preservation. The group's spokesman was Hazen Sise, consulting Heritage Planner for the National Capital Commission.

Like mourners paying their last respects, heritage advocates, still fighting to save the chapel of the Convent of Our Lady of the Sacred Heart, gather before the altar on 28 April 1972.

2

Keenly interested in heritage buildings, Sise drafted the first paper emphasizing the architectural value of the complex. In December, the convent's future seemed assured when the promoter's architect submitted a project for a gallery of boutiques, to be laid out in the old buildings and the inner courtyard.[6] But the situation took a turn for the worse in the spring of 1972 when a scheme devised by the National Capital Commission to buy the buildings and lease them back to Glenview Realty, which would carry out the renovations and operate the boutiques, fell through because it proved to be too costly for the developer.[7] There immediately appeared an alternative plan to replace the convent complex with two 15-storey office towers. Although the press campaign to save the buildings continued, the National Capital Commission could see no way out, as it had neither the legal nor the financial means to stop the threatened demolition. At the same time, it was clarifying its position on the heritage and architectural interest of the convent. On 7 April 1972, Hazen Sise offered a compromise:

> *Without in any way denigrating the heritage value of the convent as a whole, there is absolutely no question but that the* interior of the chapel *is overwhelmingly the most important element because it is almost certainly unique, at any rate in Canada. Therefore, even if the convent must be demolished, a special effort must be made to preserve the chapel – if necessary by dismantling the interior elements with a view to recreating the chapel in some other or future structure for some worship or some other adaptive use.*[8]

On Friday 21 April, the demolition permit was issued, and Barry Padolsky announced that representatives of the citizens' groups would meet on the weekend to try to seek an injunction.[9] On 25 April, however, the wrecker's axe fell on the convent.

On 26 April, reinforcing Hazen Sise's statement of over two weeks before, the Historic Sites and Monuments Board of Canada said that:

> *The Rideau Street Convent building itself has no national historic or architectural significance, but . . . the chapel interior* is *of national significance on architectural grounds and the owners should be encouraged to preserve it if at all possible.*[10]

The Board refused to place a heritage plaque on the chapel, because the building was eligible for heritage status only if it remained on its original site. However, the tentative designation of the interior, granted by the Hon. Jean Chrétien on 26 April, was confirmed two days later. It was therefore a deeply symbolic gesture when members of A Capital for Canadians, the Citizens' Committee for Planning in Sandy Hill – including core members of Action Sandy Hill – and the Save the Convent committee went to the chapel on 28 April to lay a commemorative plaque with the following inscription:

> *This plaque is erected by some citizens of Ottawa to mark the honour which the Government of Canada has accorded to this sacred place on the eve of its destruction.*[11]

The same day, Pierre Benoit, the mayor of Ottawa, asked the demolition team for a reprieve. He then called together all the parties in a final effort at mediation to save the chapel in situ.[12] An agreement could not be reached, however, and on 6 May, at 2 a.m., while most of Ottawa slept, the wrecker's ball struck the main walls of the convent, reducing it to rubble by the morning. The chapel still stood.[13] On 12 May the NCC announced that an operation to salvage the interior of the chapel had

On 28 April 1972, the chapel interior was designated as being of heritage significance by the Hon. Jean Chrétien. A youthful supporter signs her name beside a plaque placed on the chapel by citizens' groups. The building itself could not be saved, though the designated interior was dismantled and preserved. The symbolic candle is held by Mary Anne Phillips, a member of the Heritage Committee of A Capital for Canadians.

3

Cartoon by Rusins Kaufmanis on the editorial page of *The Ottawa Citizen,* 21 April 1972, the day the demolition permit was issued for the convent.

4

been launched, thanks to the collaboration of the National Gallery of Canada, which undertook to buy it at a price equivalent to the cost of the salvage operation.[14] The work of dismantling the chapel was finished by the end of May.

Although the heritage groups were unable to stop the demolition of the convent, the chapel's architectural decor was saved. Not only were all of its pieces collected – 1,123 items unfastened or sawn off – but the length of the public debate also allowed students from Algonquin College to make measured drawings of the whole. In addition, profes-

The morning after. Demolition crews in the early morning of 6 May 1972 levelled the main buildings of the convent. Still standing in the rear is the brick wing built in 1873–74, with the stone-walled chapel to the left. The site of the chapel, so coveted by the developers, today contains only a two-storey commercial building and a parking lot.

5

A wide opening is punched in the long side of the chapel building facing Besserer Street, to permit the dismantling and removal of the vault fans.

6

sional staff from Parks Canada (then in the Department of Indian Affairs and Northern Development), with the cooperation of the National Research Council, were able to make a photogrammetric survey of the endangered masterwork to facilitate the task of reassembly and restoration when the time came.[15]

The unfortunate affair had some happy consequences in other respects as well. The energy mobilized to save this important work of architecture led to the birth in 1973 of the Heritage Canada Foundation, whose purpose is to promote the understanding and preservation of Canada's heritage, and to a marked quickening of interest in many fields of heritage conservation, involving activity in local neighbourhoods, governments, business, and the related professions.

Dismantling the interior decor, May 1972. The vault is cut away and the fans are brought down one after the other, revealing the structure of the building.

One spectacular aspect of the salvage operation was the transporting of the vault fans. The great cones of carved wood crossed Ottawa on big trailers, drawing the attention of curious onlookers and the news media.

7   8

On 15 June 1973 the National Gallery became the official owner of the formidable jigsaw puzzle of fragments being stored in a warehouse on the outskirts of Ottawa. Early the following year, the newspapers were commenting on the possible reconstruction of the chapel interior in the new Gallery, then expected to open in 1980.[16] When the project for the new building was put back, there was thought for a time of reinstalling the chapel in the Lorne Building, on Elgin Street, which the National Gallery had occupied since 1960, but the idea was soon dismissed because of the scale and estimated cost of the work.

The dismantled chapel was then forgotten; indeed, it was left out of the proposal for a new Gallery building when it resurfaced in 1983. However, in February 1984 the government announced that steps had been taken to accommodate the chapel in the new building. This marked the beginning of studies and appraisals that have culminated in the restoration of the architectural decor and its integration into a new space where it can again be seen by the public.

An Exhibit in a Gallery – or a Gallery Chapel?

It is relatively rare to find works of architecture housed in museums, and with good reason. Collecting works of this type is no easy task; it is one that at times may even be meaningless, insofar as a building's site is an integral part of its history and significance. Hence, most international documents and conventions on conserving architectural heritage ban the moving or displacing of historic buildings, or portions thereof.

In this instance, the National Gallery of Canada, the owner (by force of circumstance) of part of the structure – a carved wood interior – undertook to display it in its new building. But how? Should the chapel of the Convent of Our Lady of the Sacred Heart be rebuilt on the Gallery grounds, or should its interior be regarded as an architectural work to be exhibited or somehow hung on the walls of a room, somewhat like a painting, drawing, or architect's plan?

Museums of architecture are not legion, and those that have appeared in recent decades exhibit drawings, plans, and models rather than actual architecture. In some large museums, however, works of architecture can be found. For example, The Cloisters, administered by the Metropolitan Museum of Art in New York, is a composite collection of buildings and portions of medieval architecture as well as a museum. Completed in 1938 in a park on the heights overlooking the Hudson River, the building has been constructed with original items brought back to the United States by the sculptor George Grey Bernard and complemented by accompanying architecture that is modern, yet of a compatible antique style.[17]

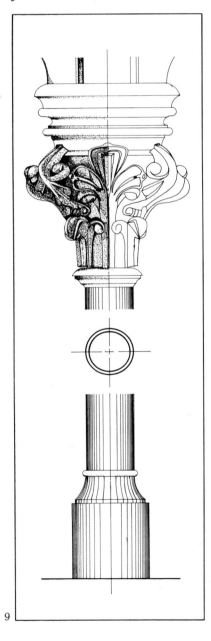

Detail of a cast-iron column, with its capital, from one of the drawings prepared in the survey done by students of Algonquin College in June 1971.

9

The Metropolitan Museum also exhibits works of architecture within its precincts in Central Park. A complete Egyptian tomb sits imposingly in the centre of a vast, light-filled room, reminiscent of a monumental sculpture by a great master. A little farther off, the neoclassical façade of a bank rises before the entrance to the American Art rooms. Here, the work is hung, somewhat like a picture on a wall, except that the entrance door actually serves as such and the base of the façade rests on the ground.

More common are "period rooms," which reconstruct in considerable detail the interiors typical of bygone centuries. Such rooms

One of the pictures taken during the photogrammetric survey by Parks Canada and the National Research Council, showing the choir woodwork shortly before dismantling.

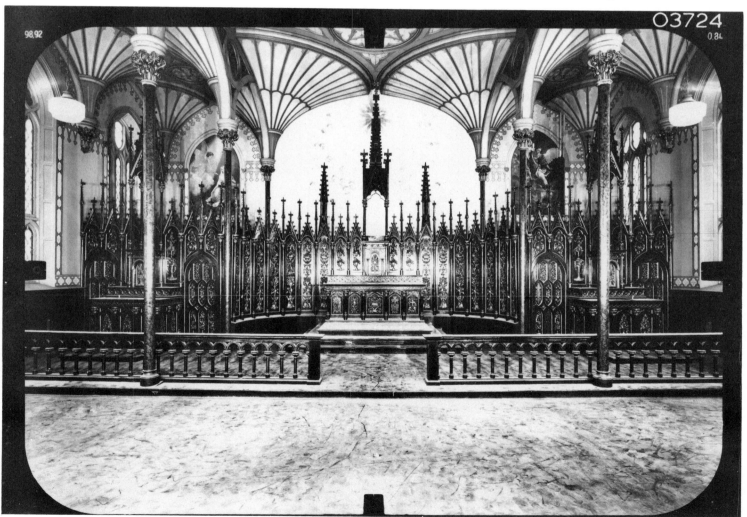

are valuable in a specific old house, castle, or public building, but when placed in a museum they are mere reconstructions of mainly educational interest. Consequently they are no longer set up in art museums, now that audiovisual technology can recreate such artificial aggregations at less cost, with more evocative power, and without compromising the nature of the artifacts being used.

On the other hand, there have been frequent attempts to incorporate into museums authentic, complete interiors that have been saved from demolition. The Landsdowne Room, for example, an eighteenth-century London work by the architect Robert Adam, thus found its way to the Philadelphia Museum of Art in 1931.[18] A careful restoration has drawn recent attention to this method, while raising more questions about its limitations. Should such a room be refurnished? If so, how? If not, of what use is it empty?

Canadian expertise in this area was limited when the National Gallery was entrusted with the task of integrating the interior of

In photogrammetry, many pictures are collated to reconstruct the whole and execute the plan. Seen here is the ceiling of the nave and side aisles. The reference numbers on the fans were assigned during the photogrammetry process.

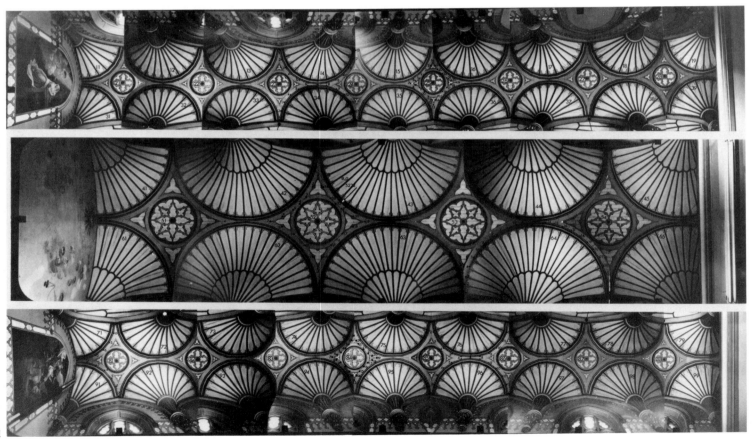

11

the chapel of the Rideau Street Convent. Museums in Canada are younger than their counterparts in the United States and Europe, and interest in architectural conservation is relatively more recent. However, we do have some historic villages in Canada, comparable to the open-air museums of northern Europe. The most famous of these is Upper Canada Village in Ontario, which features a collection of buildings threatened by the construction of the St. Lawrence Seaway in 1956. Elsewhere, as in the Port-Royal habitation and the fortress of Louisbourg in Nova Scotia, much more reconstruction than restoration has gone into the sites, where objects are displayed that illustrate life in Canada at a given moment in history.

More rare are the instances in which works have been taken down for reassembly elsewhere, particularly in a museum. In the sixties a heritage building, the Hôtel-de-France, in Montreal's Place d'Armes was dismantled for this purpose but the stones were later lost. The Musée du Québec has considered reassembling the reredos of the seventeenth-century Church of l'Ange-Gardien within its walls, but the difficulties of the undertaking have yet to be surmounted. In short, the reconstruction of the interior of the Sisters of Charity's chapel in Ottawa is proving to be a first in the history of architectural conservation in Canada – a fact that should be emphasized.

After the 1984 decision to install the work in the National Gallery, a task force reviewed a number of integration alternatives in terms of the problems posed by the very nature of the elements preserved.[19]

Although it was clearly worthwhile to have saved this architectural interior, even though the structure that housed it had been demolished, it was also obvious that the work required a framework to accommodate it. The task was made more complex in that the main part of the work is a vault, an element which defines a space – the space it covers – much more than it does a surface. If it was impossible to hang this vault on a wall of the Gallery, it was even less possible to hang it on the ceiling, leaving open space around it. Few visitors would have appreciated the qualities of this canopy defining the space below, because the vault alone would not suffice to identify it as belonging to a chapel: many secular nineteenth-century buildings, especially in England, were decorated in this way.[20] However, the ambiguity is removed if the choir woodwork and high altar are added. This immediately raised another question: why not rebuild the entire chapel down to the last minute detail?

This alternative was rejected fairly quickly, chiefly because the role of the National Gallery is to present works and not contexts, whether they are made of authentic objects or not.

In the warehouse, workmen Dennis Carr (left) and Craig Simms move a roundel of the chapel ceiling into place, carefully matching saw cuts made during the dismantling process. This was one of three preassembly techniques tested in the warehouse before the actual Gallery installation took place. The reassembly of the vault fans was the most complex operation in the restoration. The damage caused by hasty dismantling had to be repaired while the wooden fragments, which had been conserved separately for some fifteen years, were fitted together. Then the unity of the work was restored by means of subtle touch-ups designed to conceal the holes left in the dismantling process.

12

In terms of principles, the issue seemed a simple one – except that restoration of the various parts of the preserved interior posed the same problems again from a different point of view. If the sections of the vault were installed in a space that reproduced the measurements of the

The installation of the architectural decor of the chapel of the Rideau Street Convent as it appeared in the National Gallery in December 1987.

13

demolished chapel and the sanctuary woodwork was added, to what extent should all these elements be restored? They had deteriorated from the effects of hasty disassembly and twelve years of storage, and the damage had to be repaired. Was the chapel to be returned to its state on 25 June 1888 when it was dedicated, or to the state of its first redecoration in 1910, or to that of its second in 1944?[21] As a final alternative, why not restore it to its condition just before demolition?

Each of these possible courses of action had its advantages and, of course, its disadvantages. The earlier the date selected, the more difficult is the research and the more inferences have to be made. On the other hand, the later the date selected, the more observable are the facts and, an important factor, the less danger there is in altering, irreversibly, the preserved parts of the work – as might occur, for example, in searching for the first layer of paint.

In collaboration with a team from the Canadian Parks Service (then Parks Canada) and with the assistance of consultants from Commonwealth Historic Resource Management Limited, the Gallery authorities finally opted for restoration of the last existing state of the chapel interior. Architect Bouillon's work is therefore exhibited as a work of art in a museum setting, sufficiently complete to be intelligible, but permanently detached from its context.

The restoration has thus attempted to fill in gaps in the work caused during the dismantling process and to reestablish its continuity, while respecting the traces of time. It is the third and last state that is being exhibited – the one that heritage advocates wanted to save – and the signs of age have been retained. The work has not been repainted or regilded, as is too often the case with hasty restorations that do violence to the image of authenticity conferred by the patina, the mark of aging.

To ensure the clearest possible presentation of a work whose polychromy and sculptured motifs contrast strongly with modern architectural spaces shorn of unnecessary decoration, the restoration team opted for the recreation of certain elements in the appropriate style. Thus, some stencilled ornaments were reproduced and the wooden floor and dado were replaced. In the interests of authenticity, the old window sashes, dating from the 1920s, were placed in new pointed-arch frames, backlit to simulate daylight.

If for some the restoration should have entailed recreation of the chapel down to the smallest detail, others doubtless thought that it would have been better to limit it to essentials – that is, the restoration of the fan vaulting, the columns, and the altar, without attempting to establish a link between the work and its new envelope. The choice of the restoration group was a compromise, in which authenticity was safeguarded because the additions were reversible.

The chapel on display in the Canadian Galleries is sufficient unto itself, though the space it occupies can admit other exhibits without detracting from the distinctiveness of the whole – a work of rare quality, rich in meaning, and of an uncommon historical density.

II

A MASTERWORK ON DISPLAY

The chapel of the Convent of Our Lady of the Sacred Heart in Ottawa was built as a place of Roman Catholic worship. This initial purpose, which determined its general form and the manner of its ornamentation, remains the most important factor in interpreting the work displayed in the National Gallery of Canada. No longer serving its original purpose, the interior of the chapel has become a work of architecture that is exhibited for its inherent, distinctive qualities and for its significance, past and present.

The Convent Chapel:
A Particular Genre of Nineteenth-century Architecture
A chapel differs from a church only in that it fulfills specific functions instead of the general requirements of a parish. Chapels are therefore owned by private individuals or communities, or serve funerary or processional purposes. If they are usually smaller than churches, this is because the parish often has more substantial financial means than a smaller group – religious or other.

The religious communities of New France provided themselves at first with inner chapels for their own worship requirements. These were small oratories, relatively modest places in one of the rooms of the institution. But to meet the needs of their clientele – such as students and the sick – they soon had to erect larger chapels. These were divided into two sections. A single sanctuary opened on one side onto the outer chapel, which received those people served by the institution and the general public, and on the other side onto the choir, intended for the religious community itself. In communities of cloistered women – the Augustine Sisters of Mercy and the Ursulines in Quebec City, for example – the nuns' choir is in itself a true chapel.[1]

These outer chapels assumed the air of small churches, for they were detached from the convent and seemed like separate buildings. At the beginning of the nineteenth century, they were called upon to compensate for the paucity of parish churches, which were too few in number to serve the rapidly growing urban population. Many were given the status of succursal (or subsidiary) churches. About 1850, the Roman Catholic Church of Lower Canada began an unprecedented construction drive, and in a hierarchical reorganization endowed the

The chapel of the nursing sisters of Hôtel-Dieu in Quebec City obtained the status of a church immediately upon its construction in 1800. Its form – freestanding, with bell-tower – and its interior decor differ from the architecture of the chapels of the period.

14

The interior chapel in the Séminaire de Québec, designed in 1821 by Thomas Baillairgé (1791–1859).

15

This photograph of May 1879 shows the first chapel of the Convent of Our Lady of the Sacred Heart in Ottawa, built on the second floor of the old Mathews Hotel, Rideau Street.

16

territory with new dioceses and new parishes. The division of parishes, especially in urban areas, became so frequent that it monopolized the citizens' resources. The bishops then intervened, permitting the many new religious communities serving the needs of the urban industrial society to build only inner chapels. They were required to reserve their places of worship for their own purposes and to refrain from competing with the parish churches. This rule was more rigorously applied in the women's communities, which had a chaplain,[2] whereas the male religious orders were composed of ordained priests who were permitted to serve a parish.

The second half of the nineteenth century thus saw an increase in the number of large chapels located inside convent buildings, their existence signalled to the outside world only by the high windows required for adequate lighting. A first example of the type of chapel included in the structural layout of a building was in the Séminaire de Québec.[3] Over the years, the chapels would become bigger, as new building techniques permitted walls to be pushed farther back, ceilings to be raised, and windows to be enlarged. As early as 1869, when the Ottawa order of Grey Nuns of the Cross moved to Rideau Street, they built such a chapel on the second floor of the old Mathews Hotel,[4] simply

The mother house of the Grey Nuns of the Cross, now the Sisters of Charity, founded in Ottawa in 1845. At the centre of the building fronting on Sussex Street, seen here in its original form, is the chapel wing, built from 1882 to 1885 to the plans of Georges Bouillon.

by removing partitions and replacing them with cast-iron support columns. In 1881 the nuns entrusted Father Georges Bouillon with the task of drawing up plans for a new chapel for their mother house on Sussex Street. To provide plenty of room, it was decided in 1882 "to take two floors for the chapel."[5] This, plus the installation of side galleries, helped make the new space seem more like a church than a classroom.

The chapel of the Convent of Our Lady of the Sacred Heart thus represents a fairly characteristic style of architecture. The rectangular

Chapel of the mother house of the Grey Nuns of the Cross, Ottawa, as it appeared about 1930. Designed by Georges Bouillon in 1881, the interior was altered during renovations in the 1960s.

18

plan, with the long side of the chapel following the main wall of the building, the space divided into a nave and two side aisles by structural columns, and the high windows allowing in generous light and indicating the presence of a chapel to the outside world – all are elements common to such structures between 1875 and 1920.

These chapels in most instances – as in the convent of the Congrégation de Notre-Dame in Montreal (1874) or of the Ursulines in Roberval (1907) – were located on the upper floors, as a result of which their vaults, often semicircular or dome-shaped, could rise into the roof. The Rideau Street structure, however, had above it an attic storey containing a dormitory; its ceiling was therefore flat. In addition, the chapel wing was located at one end of the complex, where other buildings were expected to be added, and there was therefore no question of installing an exterior sacristy, or vestry for the officiating priest. Since custom dictated that the main entrance had to be located on the street and on the side opposite the sanctuary, it was impossible to place the sacristy anywhere else but inside the chapel walls.

Father Bouillon thus had to deal with constraints of this order in drawing up the chapel plan in 1887. The result, which can be seen today in the National Gallery of Canada, was an original composition that exploited to new advantage a space that was in itself somewhat commonplace.

Fan Vaulting: A Singular Solution

Even before construction began on the chapel of the Rideau Street Convent, the interior planned by Father Bouillon was an object of attention. No sooner was he reported to be the chapel architect than it was eagerly added that "the vault is in the Tudor style and execution of the plan promises . . . one of the most beautiful chapels in the land."[6]

The architect had in fact planned the building with the chapel interior in mind. The fan vault technique permitted him the liberty of placing the chapel under a dormitory, and he planned to install cast-iron columns of the desired height for his fan-vaulted ceiling. He also planned a special decor for the sanctuary that could incorporate a vestry for the officiating priest, knowing that it would not be possible to have an external sacristy.

The fan vault as a mode of interior covering was developed in Britain between 1430 and 1540, at the end of the Gothic Middle Ages. Built of stone, this type of vault is composed of an assembly of vault-units shaped like fans. These conical elements provide passage from a horizontal plane to a point of support, the capital, via rigorously symmetrical curved lines. These primary arcs, equal in length, are broken by circles, or horizontal rings, in relief. Circular in shape, these conical units are integrated with circular or partly circular patterns on the ceiling, which also appear in relief.[7]

Of all Gothic vaults, the fan vault is the form that most exploits the technology born out of use of the pointed arch. It proposes a structure – the ribs – supporting a stone ceiling whose weight is transferred to the columns and walls. When it first appeared, this type of vault was a feature of the "Perpendicular" style, a typically English ornamental scheme that provided a geometrical grid for the decorative exuberance

The inner chapel of the Sisters of the Congrégation de Notre-Dame, Montreal, in 1874.

19

This sectional view of the architectural decor of the chapel of the Rideau Street Convent indicates the extent to which the flattened profile of the fan vault matched the flat ceiling of the upper floor. Detail from one of the drawings prepared in the architectural survey by students of Algonquin College in June 1971.

20

of an architecture which, having nothing more to prove in terms of technology, was becoming sculpture.

The fan vault allowed the English master workmen of the fifteenth and sixteenth centuries to create very ornate, almost flat, stone ceilings. It was probably the impossibility of raising a rounded vault that led Georges Bouillon to this mode of covering for the chapel of Our Lady of the Sacred Heart. Aside from this type of constraint, however, his choice was not insignificant. In Gothic architecture, the Perpendicular style is a formal arrangement that is recognized as typically British, and most notably a feature of the reign of Henry VII, the founder of the Tudor dynasty. Fan vaults were in fact the last properly Gothic works to be erected before 1534, when Henry VIII proclaimed the Act of Supremacy designating himself head of the Church of England. It is therefore significant to see Georges Bouillon, building a Roman Catholic chapel in 1887–88 in Ottawa, and returning to an architectural style associated with the last hurrah of Catholicism in Britain. It can be seen as his way of paying tribute to that world, which he appreciated – and as his letters prove – while at the same time remaining consistent with a religious

Floor plan of the chapel showing, lower left, the irregular angle formed by the intersection of Waller and Besserer Streets and the corner staircase providing access from the ground floor. The choir and sacristy area, extreme right, is separated from the body of the chapel by the wooden altar screen.

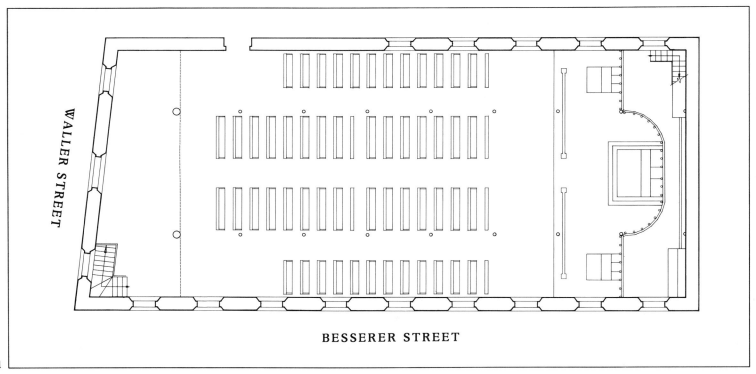

WALLER STREET

BESSERER STREET

21

commitment that led him to oppose in no uncertain terms (again revealed in his correspondence) all non-Catholic religious groups.[8]

But the Tudor vaulting, while much appreciated by the nuns running a bilingual institution, did not meet with unanimous approval. When Georges Bouillon proposed a similar style of decoration for the Mattawa church in 1888, the superior of the Oblate Fathers responded curtly that "it's very ugly for a church."[9] When the chapel of the Rideau Street Convent was consecrated, the Ottawa French-language newspaper *Le Canada* also expressed some reservations; one can read between the

The interior of the chapel of the Rideau Street Convent, as photographed by W.J. Topley in the 1890s. The trompe-l'oeil fresco behind the altar creates the illusion of a semicircular apse.

22

lines the writer's feelings about the relevance of such a work in a Catholic place of worship:

> *The convent chapel is a little building, somewhat original and rather attractive. Its style is quite rare in this country. The finest existing monument of this type, to our knowledge at least, is Westminster Abbey. While the treasury of the Kings of England was not available to the Grey Nuns, their chapel is nonetheless pretty, without being pretentious.*[10]

A number of authors have tried to establish a link between this interior – especially the vaulting – and specific models.[11] For example, it has been argued that, during his visit to England in 1883, Georges Bouillon must have seen the most famous fan vaults; those in King's College Chapel, Cambridge, and in Henry VII's Chapel in Westminster Abbey have been mentioned on several occasions as likely models. But while it is possible, and indeed probable, that the architect-priest visited these buildings – and assuredly many others with such

The stone ceiling of St. Stephen's Cloister in London, today part of the Houses of Parliament at Westminster, is a beautiful fan vault built between 1526 and 1529. This type of vault is the closest to that designed by Georges Bouillon in 1887 for the chapel of the Rideau Street Convent in Ottawa.

23

vaults[12] – this is no justification for concluding that a few years later he was capable of sitting down alone in front of his drawing board and reproducing their shape and structure.

Fan vaults were widely popularized in the early nineteenth century through various publications. The English were quick to regard Perpendicular Gothic – and thus its most perfect expression, the fan vault – as their national style, and they attempted to entrench it by proposing that its formal principle be reemployed in a neo-Gothic architecture that would therefore be equally national in character. Hence this was the style adopted by Sir Charles Barry for the reconstruction of the Houses of Parliament at Westminster, destroyed by fire in 1834. Georges Bouillon certainly had access to the many works promoting this style at the time, with illustrations giving precise reproductions of the most famous fan vaults.[13] It can be affirmed that he consulted the *Revue Générale de l'Architecture et des Travaux Publics,* the first periodical devoted to the art of construction, which was well known to all

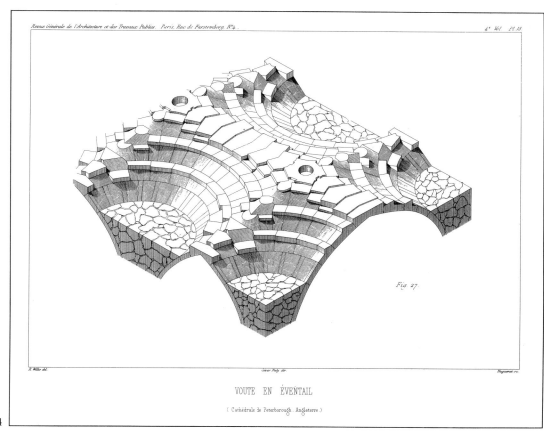

This drawing of a stone fan vault in Peterborough Cathedral, England, illustrates the construction technique employed for such vaults.

architects working in Lower Canada. In the 1843 number, the editor of the journal, architect César Daly, presents a discussion of Gothic vaulting, including a paper on fan vaults by R. Willis in a translation from the English.[14] In addition to listing twenty-seven medieval vaults, Daly refers to a publication which provides engravings of them.[15] His paper is moreover illustrated with five engraved plates showing some celebrated examples – the vaults of St. George's Chapel in Windsor and Henry VII's Chapel in Westminster Abbey – and their principle of construction.

However, these articles and plates describe medieval vaults, built in stone by a corbelling process. The chapel designed by Georges Bouillon, on the other hand, was only a decor, and its vault a pseudo-vault in wood which simply imitated an old system. It was a neo-Gothic work or, alternatively, a neo-Tudor decor, since it readopted in 1887 a decorative scheme from the years 1500–1530.

The vault of the Ottawa chapel, in width, covers a nave and two side aisles and is nine bays long. Since a side aisle is the same width as a bay and half the width of the nave, Bouillon's plan is a simple modular arrangement of fan-shaped semi-cones of two different sizes: those in the nave have a radius equivalent to the diameter of the semi-cones on the sides. The same proportion is found in the quatrefoil rosette in the central spandrel. While this system is logical on paper, it results in two incongruities. First, because of the central vault, one column in two has no fan at the top; consequently, an arch appears between the bays.[16] Next, the profile of the side aisles is much more pointed than that of the nave, because the architect wanted to keep approximately the same height clearance for the three spaces. The fans in the nave in fact spread much farther than those in the side aisles, whose ribs are shorter.

This potential for modular arrangement is one of the advantages of fan vaulting, which was highly appreciated from early in the nineteenth century, as pointed out in the *Revue Générale de l'Architecture et des Travaux Publics* in 1843:

> *In fan vaults, the difficulties of adjusting the curvatures of the ribs are at once disposed of by making them all of the same curvature.* ... *[By this system] certainly the number of templets and the difficulties were greatly diminished. The construction of these fan vaults is in all examples so nearly the same that they seem to have proceeded from the same workshop.*[17]

Since such a vault could be built by multiplying identical elements – the fans – structure and ornamentation were very soon dissociated. As early as 1679, Sir Christopher Wren, the architect in charge of rebuilding the churches destroyed in the Great Fire of London of 1666, produced the plans for the church of St. Mary Aldermary with a fan vault modelled in plaster on a wooden structure. From its inception, neo-Gothic architecture was to develop this use of the fan vault.[18] The most famous examples were the St. Michael gallery of Fonthill Abbey, a fantastic structure of 1795 which no longer exists,[19] and the conservatory of Carlton House, dating from 1811–12.[20] In Scotland, architect Gillespie Graham built new Roman Catholic chapels with these vaults in 1813 and 1814. These were resoundingly successful, even influencing the construction of Anglican churches, such as St. John's Church in Edinburgh.[21]

An 1843 drawing of the fan vaulting in Henry VII's Chapel in Westminster Abbey. Both the plan and the cross-section in this example bear little resemblance to Georges Bouillon's work, even though it is of the same type. It is probably because of its great renown that this London funerary chapel has been cited as the architect's source, without there being any evidence for the claim.

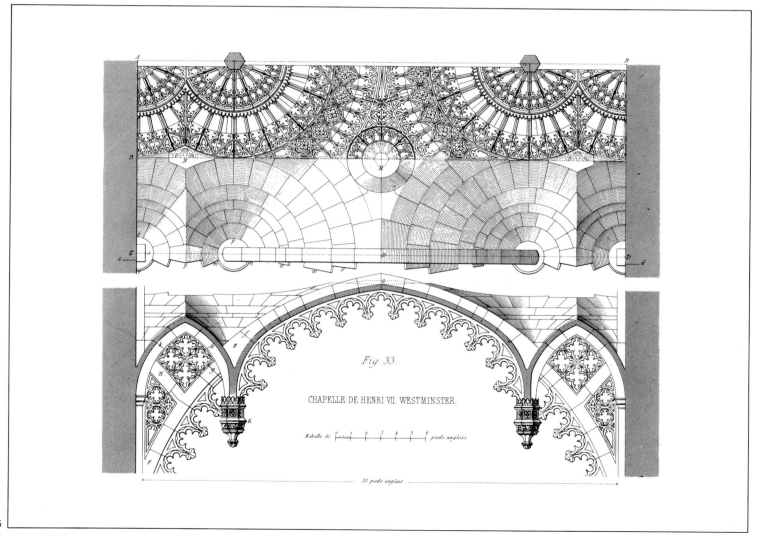

Fig. 33.

CHAPELLE DE HENRI VII, WESTMINSTER.

Echelle de 0 1 2 3 4 5 6 pieds anglais

33 pieds anglais

26

Diagram of the fan vault of the chapel of the Rideau Street Convent, prepared by Algonquin College students in 1971. This type of drawing provides a good illustration of the process of modular composition used by the architect. A square is divided into two semicircles in the nave, and in the side aisles the module is divided into four. Exactly the same system was used by Filippo Brunelleschi in 1436 for the Church of S. Spirito in Florence.

In fact, Father Bouillon could have become interested in fan vaulting through the multitude of publications that reproduced the plans of new churches, many of them built in the industrial cities of England between 1800 and 1860.[22] But there is no doubt that the vault he conceived for the Ottawa convent did not copy any of these; it is an original design from his own hand, as indeed are all his works.

But a vault alone does not create a chapel: in Roman Catholic tradition, important liturgical furnishings complete the space. Because it was incorporated into a convent, the chapel inherited a rectangular plan, typical of many Protestant churches, in which the style is more restrained. Somewhat as the architect James O'Donnell had already done for the Church of Notre Dame in Montreal in 1825, Georges Bouillon created an apse in the chapel area by installing neo-Gothic woodwork.[23] Among other things, this made room for a small sacristy below and a gallery above, accessible via a little staircase.

All of this decor was executed in wood, somewhat surprising for 1880–90 when the interiors of urban Catholic churches were generally finished in plaster, mainly for protection against fire, but also, it must be admitted, to ensure a better quality of work. This slightly "old-fashioned" use of wood might be explained by the limited financial means of the community of Grey Nuns of the Cross, but perhaps we can also see in it the expression of a certain conservatism. Father Bouillon, after all, had inherited an ecclesiastical art which, in Lower Canada, had expressed itself in quite original fashion with a rich and exuberant decor in striking contrast to the more sober style of Protestant churches. It is probably from this perspective that we should interpret all the work of this architect-priest who left his mark in an area of architecture particularly characteristic of the Roman Catholic Church – that is, the design and the appointments of the interior.

One Architect-Priest among Others

The man who produced the plans for the chapel of the Convent of Our Lady of the Sacred Heart was a priest, a member of the clergy of the diocese of Ottawa. When he began his career as an architect, about 1880, a number of architect-priests had already left their mark on the history of Canadian architecture. All of them demonstrated the Church's desire to exert better control over an architectural practice aimed at erecting places of worship and other ecclesiastical buildings.

To avoid distortion in the lines of the fans, the fan vault is generally used as a covering for buildings with a single nave, as in St. John's Church in Edinburgh, William Burn, architect, 1816. The more open space of the chapel of the Rideau Street Convent, with its side aisles, is unique in this respect.

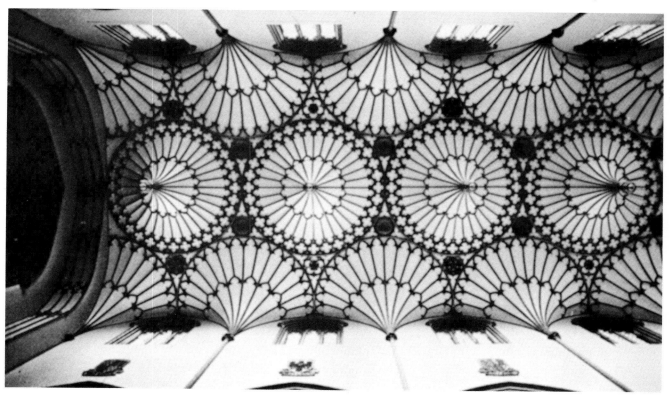

27

Although there were several priests and religious involved in art and architecture in New France – one thinks of Frère Luc, the painter and architect, or Jacques Leblond, *dit* Latour, the sculptor – their work was solely intended to serve as a stopgap for the lack of artists and architects. At the end of the eighteenth century, however, the scene was changing.

Father Pierre Conefroy (1752–1816) became interested in architecture primarily because his Boucherville parish needed a new church. The construction of his church in 1801 gave him an opportunity to codify and standardize traditional building expertise. Although his work did result in some standardization of the religious architecture of his time, it primarily regulated procedures for construction and for distributing costs among parishioners.[24]

Once this was established, the Church attempted to regain control of its architectural program by playing the supervisory role of client to the fullest. Father Jérôme Demers, priest of the diocese of Quebec City and professor of architecture at the Séminaire de Québec, redefined architectural practice so that it opened the door for lay architects – such as Thomas Baillairgé (1791–1859) – but also limited their work to the decorative element of architecture. The art of building, the heavy construction, remained the province of the master builder – the tradesman. Setting out the requirements, or establishing the architectural program, was the responsibility of the Church official – the architect-priest. The stylistic definition of the building – which in the neoclassical period (1820–50) was multifunctional, applicable to houses, banks, and prisons, as well as churches – was left to the architect. The latter,

A cross-section drawing of the chapel of the Rideau Street Convent, showing how the varying width of the spaces to be covered modifies the profile of the fans.

28

more artist than builder, in some instances might not even be a Roman Catholic, as were neither James O'Donnell nor John Ostell in Montreal.[25]

The lack of well-trained Francophone Catholic architects spurred a number of priests from among the religious communities to enter the field, especially around the middle of the nineteenth century. But the Church's needs also changed. The dioceses, now more numerous, controlled the practice of architecture through the vicar-general, the bishop's right hand, who was specifically in charge of construction. Under the vicar-general, the traditional master builder was transformed into a contractor who planned, organized, financed, and supervised the building site and the onsite workmen from the various trades. If the relations between the client and the master builder were fairly good, the lay architect, who came from outside, was less and less appreciated by the ultramontane faction[26] of the Church, which would no longer accept that Roman Catholic and Protestant churches should have uniform styles.

Father Félix Martin (1804–1886), a Jesuit, arrived from France in 1842. Initiated into architecture by his brother, a specialist in restoring Gothic churches, Félix Martin was invited to draw up proposals for several churches – including plans for the reconstruction of the Ottawa cathedral (1843) and the façade of St. Patrick's Church in Montreal (1840). In both instances it was a matter of guaranteeing the character – at least distinctive if not French – of a neo-Gothic style for use by the Canadian Church.[27] After Martin was called back to France, not without having influenced Victor Bourgeau, it was Father Joseph Michaud (1822–1902), a cleric from Saint-Viateur, who was to ensure a return to formal orthodoxy.

Since the ultramontane movement advocated the supremacy of Rome, the bishop of Montreal, Monsignor Ignace Bourget (1799–1885), attempted to impose the architecture that best evoked papal authority – the neo-Baroque style of Montreal's Église du Gésu, for example (1864–65). As a model for his cathedral, the present Basilica of Mary Queen of the World (1875–85), he unhesitatingly and with no false modesty chose St. Peter's of Rome. Victor Bourgeau, an adept in neo-Gothic architecture, was therefore removed to the background, at least while Father Michaud drew up the plans for the new building. But the cleric's role did not stop there: the bishop assigned him to help the most remote parishes in his diocese, as well as the new missions, to confer a "Roman" stamp on their traditionally styled buildings, both inside and out, however modest they might be.[28]

In a way, Georges Bouillon could be seen as completing Father Michaud's mission, in that he was active as an architect in a diocese which, about 1880–85, contained no Francophone Catholic architects.[29] But the architect-priest from Ottawa found himself with another mission, one doubtless determined by choice, but also by necessity.

More artist than builder, Georges Bouillon devoted himself more to interior decor than did his predecessors. In the tradition of the Canadian Church, this was the ideal field in which to develop an architectural vocabulary, the building itself being rather severe. The interior decor of a church simultaneously filled symbolic needs – translated into the particular disposition of space, the richness of ornament, and the iconography; it also satisfied more modestly functional needs – the arrangement of furnishings, means of access, and ease of circulation. These combined to form the essentials of a Roman Catholic church and thus helped to distinguish it from other places of worship.

This is not to say that Father Bouillon was not interested in the general plans of buildings; he executed a number of them, and all his writings imply that he would have very much liked to be named vicar-general of the diocese, mainly so that he could have better directed the Church's architectural practice in Ottawa. But his attention to detail, his penchant for ornamentation, and his aesthetic ideal distanced him from actual construction practice. Consequently, he was quite naturally to become the architect-ornamentalist that certain of the ecclesiastical hierarchy were seeking, someone to defend the identity of a Church that, as the twentieth century approached, seemed to be losing ground in a rapidly evolving society. From this standpoint, experimental as it was, the architectural work of Georges Bouillon was the equivalent of the painting being done in the studios of the Sisters of the Good Shepherd or the Sisters of Charity of Quebec. They too had been entrusted with a mission by the Church: to safeguard the sacred character of an art which lay practice was reducing solely to an aesthetic and stripping of its themes. It was precisely the religious theme that inspired Bouillon; his interior architecture was to be a kind of iconography of the spirit and influence of Christianity in the world.

Georges Bouillon was not the last architect-priest. He was succeeded, for example, by Father Jean-Thomas Nadeau (1883–1934) in Quebec City and the Benedictine monk Dom Paul Bellot (1876–1944), French by birth but active in the province of Quebec from 1934 to 1944. Nadeau strove to renew religious architecture by introducing into Quebec the rationalist doctrine, while distinguishing churches from other public buildings by adopting a neo-medieval style, taught and promoted by the École des beaux-arts in Quebec City.[30] Bellot arrived at just the right moment – that is, shortly after the Depression – to renew both the form and function of the religious architecture of Quebec; he

Construction began on the Cathedral-Basilica of Notre Dame in Ottawa in 1839. In 1843, Father Félix Martin revised the plans, and the cathedral was completed in 1845 in the neo-Gothic style, under the direction of Father Adrien Telmon, architect-priest. The two steeples were finished in 1858 to the plans of Father Damase Dandurand. A semicircular, angled choir, designed by the architect Victor Bourgeau, replaced the flat apse in 1862.

29

was, in fact, inspired by the liturgical revival at the time, aimed at a revivification of Christian art and architecture.[31]

But they, like Georges Bouillon, had to come to terms with established architects. These were protected by their professional association, which did not look kindly on the survival of client-architects that enabled the Church, as the owner, to exert control over the image it wished to project through its buildings.

The Aesthetics of Georges Bouillon:
Eclecticism at the Service of the Church
The chapel of the Convent of Our Lady of the Sacred Heart was not Canon Bouillon's only work, even if the attention it has gained in being incorporated into the National Gallery of Canada might temporarily

Georges Bouillon designed the interior of the Church of Saint-François-de-Sales in Gatineau in 1901, seen here in an old photograph from the parish archives. The fans in this decor are secondary motifs, pendentives, which link the main coffered ceiling with the lateral and transverse arches.

30

overshadow his other accomplishments. However, an examination of these works, the Canon's writings, and a brief reminder of the context in which art and architecture developed during this era will show the interior of the chapel of the Rideau Street Convent in a different light, and explain it, not as an isolated phenomenon, but as a work that reveals the consistency of its designer's activity and its place in the context of an era.

First, the style adopted for this chapel is not unique in Georges Bouillon's work. Although his proposed plan to include fan vaulting in the church of Sainte-Anne in Mattawa was rejected in 1888, in 1901 he succeeded in providing the Church of Saint-François-de-Sales in Gatineau (then Pointe-Gatineau) with this type of ornamentation. These two interiors, though similarly inspired, are yet so different that the

Detail of the vault of the Church of Saint-François-de-Sales in Gatineau.

31

hand of the same architect cannot positively be recognized at first. Indeed, there are sufficient disparities between the decor of the chapel of the Rideau Street Convent and that of the Gatineau church to make it clear that the designer was pursuing variety much more than he was emphasizing continuity.

One reaches the same conclusion in examining other examples of the architect-priest's major works: in fact, nothing seems more incoherent or more heterogeneous than a collection of Bouillon's interiors. Consider the magnificent neo-Gothic decor of the Ottawa cathedral, much influ-

The interior of the Church of Notre Dame in Montreal, as photographed by William Notman about 1880. Completed to the plans of architect Victor Bourgeau, starting in 1876, this work, like Bourgeau's architecture in general, played a major role in the career of Georges Bouillon. It was Bourgeau, in fact, who translated neo-Gothic into terms acceptable to the Roman Catholic Church by creating a synthesis between established tradition (wood decor, rich ornamentation) and a new formal repertoire (Gothic arches, polychromy, subdued atmosphere). He renewed ties with the great models of French Gothic, brought into its own by nineteenth-century architect-restorers who wanted to see a return to the starry vaults and gilded polychromy of the monumental buildings of the twelfth and thirteenth centuries.

32

enced by that of the Church of Notre Dame in Montreal; the chapel (now destroyed) of the University of Ottawa, exotic enough for historians to have described it as Mozarabic; the very different baldachins of the churches in Bic and Rimouski; or the sumptuous interior of the church in Trois-Pistoles. There seems to be no common denominator in all of this, except the eclectic taste of the architect.

Eclecticism was a nineteenth-century movement in architectural history. It borrowed the best elements of the various formal systems of the past to create the "nineteenth-century style."

The Cathedral of Notre Dame in Ottawa, for which Georges Bouillon designed the interior decor in 1876–82. The influence of Victor Bourgeau is evident here, in features such as the small clustered columns, the ornamentation of the gallery balustrades, and the design of the mouldings. Even though the two buildings are dissimilar in structure, their internal ambiance and quality of space are much the same.

33

The reredos and choir stalls of the Cathedral of Notre Dame in Ottawa. This intricately executed woodwork is evidence of the decisive influence of Victor Bourgeau on Georges Bouillon's art, an influence so strong that it is possible the Montreal architect may have helped Father Bouillon design these furnishings, which were undertaken at the same time as those in the Church of Notre Dame in Montreal.

Several traits characterized this new style. First, eclecticism resulted from the exercise of many choices – for example, according to requirements, materials, technologies, and increased understanding of more and more varied forms. It was governed by new aesthetic criteria, with sensuous appreciation of the work replacing reasoned apprehension of the Beautiful. This "nineteenth-century style" was invested with the new obligation to convey symbolic meaning – that is, to evoke an association of ideas through form (for example, terrace = nature = villa;

34

or Gothic = English); it lost all pretensions to uniformity, characterizing itself on the contrary by variety of expression. Hence the temptation of historians to see in it as many "styles" or "manners" as there are possible categories. Thus one spoke of an architect's style as of a painter's style – the neo-Tudor style, the château style, the Beaux-Arts style, and so forth.

Georges Bouillon was initiating himself into architecture and producing his first plans when this stylistic debate was current in ecclesiastical

35

Impressed by the ancient Basilica of St. Sophia of Constantinople, Georges Bouillon dreamt throughout his career of reproducing the form in North America, just as Monsignor Ignace Bourget did his best to reproduce St. Peter's of Rome in Montreal. Consequently, to the end of his life, Bouillon was to produce plans and drawings for a *Nova Sancta Sophia* on a monumental scale. This drawing for the project dates from about 1902.

circles. Faced with the variety of artistic and architectural production and the general secularization of art, the Church was striving to create a truly Christian imagery or symbolism by proposing the great buildings of its past as models of artistic expression.

In Montreal, the architect and painter Napoléon Bourassa was earning a reputation for himself through his speeches and papers on religious art.[32] For him, faith inspired the artist, since all the great works of the past were religious in origin. Every work of art and architecture thus became a teaching of faith in God, a religion. Bourassa was very influenced by Victor Cousin, the father of French eclectic philosophy, and suggested that artists and architects take their inspiration from all the styles of the past.[33]

Canon Bouillon does not seem to have left any writings explaining his theory of art and architecture. But there are enough indications in his correspondence to establish a link with Bourassa's thought. For example, echoing Cousin, who was championed by Bourassa, he wrote that "Religion walks hand in hand with the Arts."[34] And when Bourassa praised the ancient Basilica of St. Sophia of Constantinople, Bouillon echoed: "St. Sophia, what grandeur, what magnificence in that building!"[35]

These drawings show Georges Bouillon's plans, executed in 1898, for the church in Trois-Pistoles, including the baldachin and cross-section of the church from the transept. This is a fine example of a style the architect termed "Romano-Byzantine," a synthesis of architectural forms from the first centuries of the Christian era.

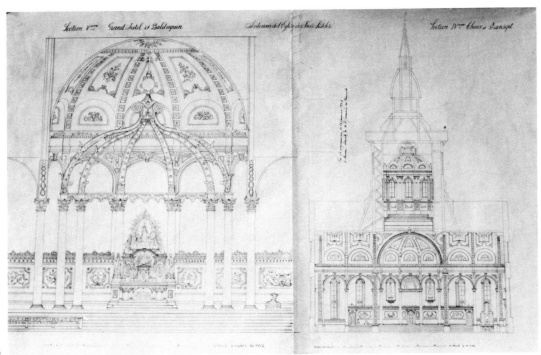

(Opposite)
The interior of the chapel of the University of Ottawa, designed by Georges Bouillon in 1887 and destroyed by fire in 1903. This decor, long termed "Mozarabic" by historians, in fact adopts the decorative scheme of Indian palaces of the seventeenth and eighteenth centuries. The supporters of the eclectic style of religious architecture claimed that Christian art could appropriate all styles because, over the centuries, the Christian faith had supplanted all other beliefs, and hence their architecture. Hindu and Persian art forms would thus have been combined in Arabian art, which itself was taken up by the Christians after the Battle of Poitiers in 732, marking the end of the Islamic threat in Europe.

CHAPTER II

Also revealing is the architect-priest's reading. In 1856 César Daly published in the *Revue Générale de l'Architecture et des Travaux Publics* an impressive essay on styles.[36] He identified the historical school, which was inspired by the Middle Ages and Antiquity; the rationalist school which by "using the powerful resources of science for the benefit of architecture" was in the process of "substituting civil engineering for architecture";[37] and universal eclecticism "which has gathered before it

37

all of humanity's aesthetic past, and is integrating it and selecting from it."[38]

The vocabulary that Bouillon used reflected this type of discourse on architectural theory. The architect-priest noted that "everything changes in this world, taste as well as character" and said that he was suffering the consequences.[39] He wanted religious architecture to give expression to this evolving society; it could not remain unchanged in a changing world. Eclecticism, or the "mixing of styles," as he termed it, allowed him to draw from certain styles of the past, those he felt served as vehicles for the strongest religious symbolism.[40] He therefore readily used the English Perpendicular style – whence the fan vaulting of the chapel of the Rideau Street Convent – and also the Romano-Byzantine.

The philosophy of architectural eclecticism justified the borrowing of all architectural forms by attributing to them a symbolic value. Thus reappropriated, these styles, in the hands of architect-priests, extended the base of a Roman Catholicism which, from Schism to Reformation, had been ceaselessly retrenching since the sixteenth century. Religious architecture then became, as of old, a missionary art, participating in the life of its time.

III

THE BIRTH OF A CHAPEL

The history of the 100-year-old buildings of the Convent of Our Lady of the Sacred Heart, Ottawa, came to an abrupt end in 1972, when the complex was demolished to make way for a commercial building and a parking lot.[1]

Yet it had all begun auspiciously.

The Convent's Beginnings

In 1845, the religious community of Grey Nuns of the Cross, founded in Montreal in 1737 by Marguerite d'Youville, delegated four sisters to the town of Bytown (which later was to become Ottawa, Canada's capital), at the request of the bishop of the diocese of Kingston, Monsignor Patrick Phelan, to open a school and take care of the sick. (The Ottawa sisters kept the name Grey Nuns of the Cross until 1964, when they reverted to the name chosen by their eighteenth-century founder: the Sisters of Charity.) Under the direction of the first superior, Mother Marie-Élisabeth Bruyère, and at the invitation of the bishop of the new diocese of Ottawa, Monsignor J.-E. Bruno Guigues, the first school opened in 1849 on St. Patrick Street.[2] The next year, in 1850, the convent of the Grey Nuns on Sussex and Bruyère Streets was ready to receive day students and boarders.

Nearly twenty years later, the success of the educational program and the increasing number being served in the infirmary and the orphanage forced the nuns to consider expansion. In May 1869, the community's general council decided to buy Thomas Mathews's property, the inn known as Revere House, described as: "located on Rideau Street, in the parish of St. Joseph, with a garden, fine yard and many good, large outbuildings and ... a large, handsome house."[3] On 2 June, the nuns signed the purchase contract for "Mr. Mathews's hotel"[4] and immediately set up a boarding and day school for girls.[5]

The block formed by Rideau, Waller, Besserer, and Cumberland Streets, Ottawa, the site of the Convent of Our Lady of the Sacred Heart.

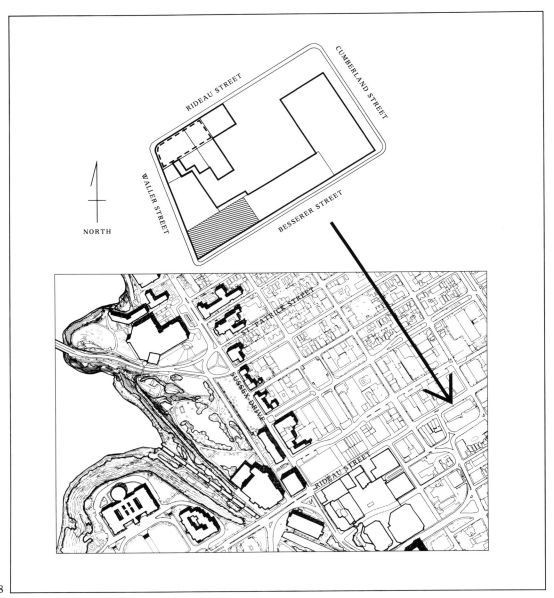

38

The block formed by Rideau, Waller, Besserer, and Cumberland Streets, where the convent stood, is closely tied to the history of Ottawa's development. Located at the boundary of Sandy Hill, so named because of the nature of its soil, this sector of Rideau Street was developed immediately after the construction of the Parliament Buildings. Starting in the 1860s, the vast estate acquired by Louis-Théodore Besserer in 1828 was developed to help accommodate the many government officials arriving in the young capital on the eve of Confederation.[6]

Probably built about 1840, Revere House was a classical vernacular building typical of the Ottawa region in the early nineteenth century, with its massed form, slightly inclined hip roof, end chimneys, and sash windows. The hotel had already been enlarged when the nuns took possession. An imposing addition had been erected on the corner of Rideau and Waller Streets about 1855 and, in a photograph from about 1865,[7] the two buildings, now joined, share a wide gallery at the second-floor level.

The nuns took up residence in September 1869 and named their school Our Lady of the Sacred Heart/Notre-Dame-du-Sacré-Coeur. Barely two years later, the institution already counted 62 boarders and 185 day students receiving instruction in both English and French. In view of this success, the nuns began to consider expansion in 1871. Recognizing that the student residence needed a new wing, the general council of the community asked the advice of Father Joseph-Henri Tabaret, rector of the University of Ottawa, who recommended building it away from Rideau Street. The nuns hesitated. Finally on 5 December 1872 they decided to stay in the same neighbourhood, "after taking counsel with his Grace, the Monsignor of Ottawa."[8] But to avoid

The Mathews Hotel in Ottawa, also known as Revere House, as it appeared about 1865, a few years before the Grey Nuns of the Cross bought it for their Convent of Our Lady of the Sacred Heart.

39

Mother Theresa of Jesus, Superior of the Convent of Our Lady of the Sacred Heart (1870–1912), in a portrait photograph by W. J. Topley. Mother Theresa commissioned the construction of the convent's remarkable neo-Gothic chapel from architect-priest Georges Bouillon. Born Martha Hagan of Irish parents in Sainte-Marie-de-Monnoir, Quebec, on 5 January 1829, she came to Ottawa (then Bytown) with her parents in 1837. Hugh Hagan, her father, was a teacher and directed a private school. From her youth, Martha Hagan was an imposing figure – wise and reserved, high-spirited and strong. She spoke English and French fluently. Entering the order of Grey Nuns of the Cross in 1847, she embarked immediately on a life of teaching. In 1870 she became Mother Superior of the convent, a position she held until her death in 1912. An inspired teacher, Mother Theresa was also an able administrator, with a decided flair for building design and construction. Her talents extended also to her mission to guide the intellectual and moral development of her house. The far-reaching fame of the Rideau Street Convent owed much to her administrative skills, her enterprising spirit, her devotion to her calling, and her innate gifts as an educator.

40

CHAPTER III

the possible unseemly distractions of Rideau Street, the southern edge of thundering, disreputable Lower Town, the "ladies'" boarding establishment was housed in a new brick wing, built in 1873–74, on the side of the block facing Waller Street.

The new wing, connected to the former hotel by a small intermediary building, was a tall structure of generous proportions containing five classrooms, three spacious, well-lit dormitories, fifteen smaller rooms, two music halls, and two waiting rooms. The oldest visual record we have of it is a photograph taken by Topley in April 1886, with a group of students posing proudly at the corner. Even at this period it is evident that the older building had undergone renovations "to make it more suitable for the pupils."[9] Hence the severe appearance of the elevation of the ground floor on Rideau Street, with its many blocked-up openings. But the nuns in 1886 were harbouring a desire "to sell Our Lady of the Sacred Heart boarding school on Rideau Street, in order to build in a better location."[10] They continued to be concerned that Rideau Street was becoming more and more a commercial artery, and that Lower Town remained a roistering working-class district that had little affinity with a college for girls.

Doubtless after consultation with the diocesan authorities, as before, the nuns abandoned their project, and in 1887 took steps to isolate themselves from an environment that they saw as little suited to their particular educational function. The general council of the community

A group of students pose in front of the Convent of Our Lady of the Sacred Heart, photographed by W. J. Topley in 1886.

41

decided "that it is more advantageous to leave the institution where it is, and to buy the neighbouring properties so that it can be enlarged and properly surrounded."[11] Instead, then, of following the example of most of the religious communities of the time and leaving the city for the suburbs, the Grey Nuns decided to remain where they were, and even to expand. They gradually acquired all the lots in the Rideau-Waller-Besserer-Cumberland block, and were thus able to raise a stone wall around their property in 1892.[12] Their long-range plan seems to have been to enclose the land with a series of buildings, and so to create a huge, private inner courtyard.

"One of the most beautiful chapels in the land"

In May 1887, the community bought the lot at the corner of Waller and Besserer Streets to even further enlarge the convent.[13] This time, the projected new wing was mainly intended to house a chapel worthy of the enviable reputation that the school had acquired in Ottawa and the region. The nun in charge of the convent's chronicles wrote in March

The chapel of the Rideau Street Convent at the corner of Waller and Besserer Streets, with the modern classroom building of 1927 to the right and the 1873–74 brick wing to the left.

42

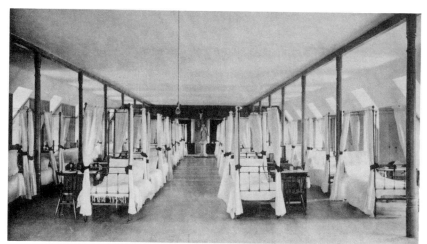

43

The top floor of the chapel of the Convent of Our Lady of the Sacred Heart housed a dormitory under the mansard roof. At centre is the chapel itself, about 1910, shortly after its redecoration. The trompe-l'oeil fresco in the apse has disappeared, to be replaced by a composition on the religious theme of the Sacred Heart of Jesus, in a blue sky, surrounded by adoring angels. On the ground floor of the four-storey building was a spacious "music hall," used for a variety of functions.

44

45

1887: "We shall be in Father Bouillon's debt for the magnificent plan he has proposed for our chapel. The vault is in the Tudor style, and execution of the plan promises to give us one of the most beautiful chapels in the land. We shall see next year at about this same time."[14]

Work began immediately.[15] In April, the foundations were dug. During the summer, "demolition and construction went ahead at the same time. . . . As the new building's outer walls were being finished, the walls separating the music halls were removed."[16] The building was covered in time for the winter, and in February 1888, it was reported in the chronicles that "we are proudly beginning to show our lovely chapel, which will be handed over to the decorator in a fortnight."[17]

To finance construction, the Grey Nuns organized a lottery in October 1887. Proceeds were to go toward paying part of the interest due on the borrowed capital, at least while the chapel was not bringing in any revenue.[18] The draw took place on 22 May 1888 and realized $700.

The chapel and convent, centre right, seen from the tower of the Church of Sacré-Coeur, looking north from Laurier Avenue in Sandy Hill. The parlour wing, completed in 1901, can be seen at the right.

46

Oblate Father Gendreau supervised the work and strove to find "the best contractors at the best price" – Mr. Gagnon for the masonry, John O'Connor for the carpentry, and Mr. Johnson for the plumbing.[19]

Even when the decorator M. E. Daley had completed his painting and gilding, the chapel was still not finished. As the writer of the chronicles assessed the work in June 1888, "Much still remains to be done on the chapel: the altars have to be gilded, the windows completed, the pews finished, the sacristy painted."[20]

Work was sufficiently advanced, however, for the consecration of the new chapel on 25 June 1888. Several newspapers published accounts of the ceremony, which was presided over by Monsignor Joseph-Thomas Duhamel, archbishop of Ottawa, with twenty-five priests as co-celebrants.[21] The *Free Press* reporter provided a brief but vivid description:

This 1927 drawing by the architect Werner Noffke shows his new classroom wing on Besserer Street, at the rear, adjoining the 1888 chapel.

47

COUVENT NOTRE-DAME
DU
SACRÉ COEUR
RUE RIDEAU OTTAWA
SOEURS GRISES DE LA CROIX

The chapel itself is a very handsome building occupying an area the whole of the new stone wing on Waller and Besserer Streets. It is situated just over the assembly hall, and its plain exterior gives no indication of its elegance and richness within. Its dimensions are 106 feet by 45 feet. It is, as presented, seated for 360, but could easily accommodate 150 more. The pews are all open, of varnished white pine trimmed with walnut. The space between them is unusually wide, as are also the kneeling boards. It is

Aerial view of the Rideau Street Convent complex, about 1960, four years before the last structure – the gymnasium – was built, filling the upper left (southeast) corner.

divided by light iron columns into a nave and two aisles. The capitals are fluted convolvulus and the ceiling spaces between them are covered with elaborate tracery. The lancet windows on each side are filled with stained glass and the whole chamber up to the windowsills is wainscoted in oak. The floor is red pine. Facing the altar is a good organ loft with ample choir accommodation. The screens of the grand and side altars, one of which is that of the Virgin and the other that of St. Joseph, are of rich design in oak and the cruciform finials reach almost to the ceiling. It is as handsome a chapel as any in the city.[22]

Built of stone, the new building had a mansard roof pierced with impressive dormer windows, in harmony with the adjacent wing that had been built in 1873–74.

The new chapel occupied the second floor of the building, which had a trapezoidal shape necessitated by the acute angle formed by the intersection of Waller and Besserer Streets. A huge music hall was laid out on the ground floor of the building and a spacious dormitory at the top. The chapel was two storeys high, and lit by lofty Gothic windows.

To free the interior space, the architect used columns instead of load-bearing partitions or division walls to support the long ceiling joists. This arrangement created on each of the three floors a large central space (the nave in the chapel) and two side spaces, or aisles, of the same height, leaving the way clear for any future partitioning. This

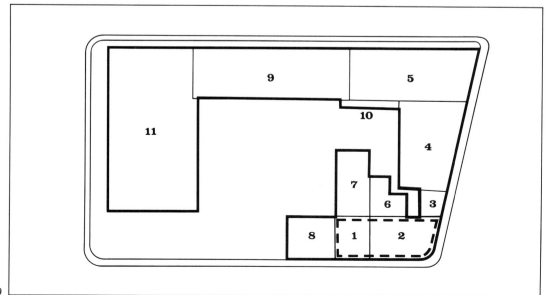

49

The stages of construction of the Convent of Our Lady of the Sacred Heart, Ottawa:
1) Revere House, about 1840
2) Mathews Hotel, about 1855
3) The connecting wing, 1873
4) The new student residence, 1873–74
5) The chapel, 1887–88
6) The kitchen, 1901
7) The refectory, 1904
8) The parlour wing, 1901
9) The classroom wing, 1927
10) The covered way, 1927
11) The gymnasium, 1964
The new roof of 1899 is indicated by a broken line.

THE BIRTH OF A CHAPEL

type of structure, developed in the middle of the nineteenth century for buildings used for trade and storage, was both economical and strong and, if the floors were solid and the ceilings plastered, provided relatively good protection against fire according to the safety standards of the time.

Because it did not require bearing walls, this building technique also allowed for variation in the height of the storeys. Hence it soon became popular for providing large public spaces inside buildings – such as reception halls, libraries, and, of course, chapels.

But at the same time, this arrangement, long considered "modern" in terms of architectural history in that it favoured the expressive use of a new type of structural support – the visible cast-iron column – called

The nave of the chapel of the Rideau Street Convent seen from the organ loft, March 1971.

50

other established features into question. First, placing these undivided rooms on top of each other created a traffic problem. How, for example, would one move around the chapel from one part of the complex to another without lateral corridors? Second, how did one develop a symbolic space, required by a specific religious function, in a building containing several storeys? The first was not a problem at the Rideau Street Convent before 1927 because the chapel was at the end of the complex. In 1927, a new block of 28 classrooms and 33 private rooms was added.[23] A covered way was then erected, a sort of exterior corridor, making it possible to move from the 1873–74 wing to the 1927 wing by skirting the outer wall of the chapel. The second question found a worthy response in the interior design of the chapel, thanks to the skill of architect Georges Bouillon.

The organ loft of the chapel over the front entrance facing Waller Street.

51

Once the erection of the chapel had completed the Waller Street façade, the community went ahead with its construction effort. In 1899 the original building on Rideau Street was raised one storey by the addition of a mansard roof.[24] Still cramped for room, the students' residence was expanded in 1901. A big new kitchen appeared behind the old Mathews Hotel, and a new wing on Rideau Street, with the same outline as the existing one, was built on part of the vacant lot to the east.[25] The spacious refectory, which appropriated space from the inner courtyard, dates from 1904.[26]

The south aisle of the chapel, looking toward the rear balcony.

52

In 1907 the nuns acquired the last vacant lot on the convent block, at the corner of Rideau and Cumberland. However, there was a pause in building activity, chiefly because of the war. The idea of leaving the area came up again on several occasions, and in 1920 the general council accepted a call option for the block and its buildings.[27] As there were no serious buyers, the nuns returned to new onsite work with the construction in 1927 of a modern building, the costs of which were partially assumed by the school board.[28] A works campaign followed to consolidate and renovate the older quarters.

The last development work took place in 1964 when a modern gymnasium was built, to the plans of architect Jean-Serge Le Fort, in the southeast corner of the block facing Besserer Street.[29] The new structure was opened on 17 May 1968, almost four years exactly before a commercial developer levelled the entire block, though not without first provoking sharp opposition from citizens' groups and other organizations. It was felt that the century of history represented by the complex should be recognized, and that the Rideau Street Convent deserved to be spared.

A Cozy Chapel – *The Ottawa Daily Citizen,*
19 May 1888

The beautiful little chapel which forms a portion of the new wing of the Rideau Street Convent is nearing completion, and it is contemplated by the contractor, Mr. John O'Connor, that within a month's time everything will be ready for the formal dedication of the pretty little unique place of worship, which will, it is most likely, be consecrated to the worship of God by His Grace Archbishop Duhamel on the 21st of June next.

A *Citizen* reporter yesterday called upon Sister Theresa, Mother Superior of the Grey Nuns' Order, under whose able and motherly direction there is a large number of lady students, several of whom will be graduated this midsummer and receive their well-merited and deserved certificates of efficiency. A courteous and kindly reception was extended by the Lady Superior, and the reporter was shown the chapel over the Music Hall of the convent, and which is in dimensions 106 feet long and 48 feet wide, and is to be heated with steam throughout.

The carpenters, the painters and the gilders were busily at work. The interior of the chapel is certainly exceedingly beautiful, the Tudor-Gothic style of ornamentation of the ceiling being a feature in the decoration which at once catches the eye. It is not gaudy or gay, nor is it the opposite extreme, but a happy medium between the two, a style which, though seldom seen in ecclesiastical architecture, is nevertheless, perhaps, as suitable for chapel ornamentation as could well be imagined. The light cobalt blue, and the fine, light pink colours blend together truly artistically, and are made the more pretty, lovely, and striking by the gold gilding of the white columns.

The walls are frescoed in oil – a new departure in chapel ornamentation, but one which adds in no small degree to the general good design. There are sixty pews, thirty each side, seven and a half feet long, made of pure walnut, oiled and varnished. The entire aisle is seven feet wide and the side aisles five feet each. The wainscoting around the chapel is ash, and the cappings of walnut. The altar, always a prominent feature in Catholic churches, or chapels, is particularly pretty, handsome and elegant in design. It is made of red cherry, and will be elaborately gilded in gold. The side altars are also made of red cherry, and, as it were, form one with the high altar. On each of the tabernacles are high pyramids, which reach almost to the ceiling.

The chapel is well lighted by some fourteen Gothic windows: there is a double set to each, the inner of stained glass and the outer of plain glass. A gallery, 44 feet wide by 11 feet long is in the far end of the church and will be fitted up with walnut balustrades, gilded and varnished. The Communion rail will also be made of the same material.

On the whole, the chapel may be said to be cozy, pretty, and elegant, and admirably adapted to the requirements of the lady students of the convent. The gilding and painting is being done by Mr. M.E. Daley, and assuredly reflects great credit on that gentleman's artistic abilities. The seating capacity is 300. It is estimated that the cost of the chapel will be in the vicinity of $20,000.

IV

GEORGES BOUILLON, ARCHITECT

He is tall, six feet, well proportioned, and stands straight as an arrow. His face and eye are kindly, and his manner is so modest and retiring that you must know his worth from seeing his work, and not from the man himself, as he makes no effort to impress you, as many another would do who had designed a simple dwelling. He is quite grey, but his face is not old. He was born a genius, as Michelangelo was born.[1]

On 7 April 1932, the Ottawa daily *Le Droit* caught its readers' attention with a large headline: "Mgr. Georges Bouillon passed away yesterday at the age of 91 years, two months."[2] The paper noted that he had been not only the doyen of all Canadian priests but also a "renowned architect" who had executed the plans for two cathedrals, an episcopal palace, and seven churches. He indeed seems to have been famous, even outside the archdiocese of Ottawa, for a number of dailies ran stories about him.[3] The biographical information revealed in these articles brought to public notice the career and accomplishments of a figure who, like the nineteenth century to which he belonged, had already been largely forgotten.

Although a few publications sponsored by the Church subsequently referred to the life and work of one of its distinguished members,[4] historians of art and architecture have been little impressed with the work of Canon Georges Bouillon. In *L'Architecture en Nouvelle-France,* published in 1949, Gérard Morisset placed him in the category of "amateur" architects who practised the profession "by necessity." Although he admits that Bouillon gave evidence of talent, he indicates that it was only in "a few works."[5] In *Hallowed Walls,* in 1975, Marion MacRae and Anthony Adamson refer to Bouillon as "a designer of interior space whose skill in handling the rich *passé* palate of early Gothic was equalled only by the immensity of his proposed budgets."[6]

The installation of one of Canon Bouillon's major architectural works in the National Gallery of Canada is a most appropriate occasion for a reappraisal of the career of Georges Bouillon, architect.

Canon Georges Bouillon (1841–1932), in a photograph of about 1900.

53

The Search for a Vocation

The name of Georges Bouillon begins to figure in the history of architecture from 1877, when it was his humble task to revise the plan for the appointments in the side galleries of the Cathedral of Notre Dame in Ottawa, where he had served as parish priest for a year.[7] Having thus demonstrated his skills, Father Bouillon received the support of his bishop, Monsignor Joseph-Thomas Duhamel, in being named supervisor of the interior decor of the mother church of the diocese from 1878 to 1883. He has left detailed accounts of the work he accomplished in this period, written in his own hand, with uncommon precision.[8]

Georges Bouillon was born on 11 February 1841, the tenth child in the family of a Rimouski farmer.[9] Nothing in his early years seems to have suggested that the young man would pursue a career in architecture. He must have attended elementary school in his parish and then the Rimouski college-seminary, which in 1854 was in its infancy. No doubt encouraged by the ecclesiastical authorities of his diocese, he went to Montreal in August 1858 to register as a postulant at the Institute of the Brothers of Christian Schools.

The Brothers of Christian Schools arrived in Montreal in 1837 at the invitation of Monsignor Jean-Jacques Lartigue. They devoted themselves to general instruction and to training teachers for elementary schools,

54

In 1867, while Georges Bouillon was living in Rimouski, where he completed his classical studies at the college-seminary, he drew this picture of his home town, titled *Village de Rimouski.*

especially in rural areas.[10] The young Bouillon, who was now known as Brother Gelasian, took the habit of the "Ignorantines"[11] on 2 October 1858 and was quick to finish his novitiate. He began working as a schoolteacher on 20 December that same year, probably under the direction of a more experienced brother, so that he could study during the summer months.[12]

After seven years with the Institute in Montreal, notably as a teacher at the École Saint-Jacques, Georges Bouillon emerged from anonymity.

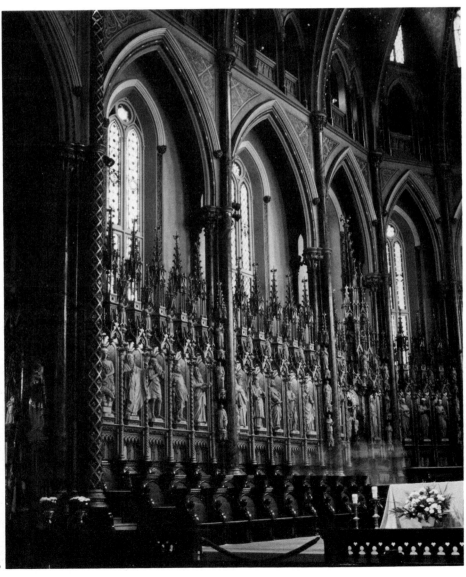

Interior of the Cathedral of Notre Dame in Ottawa. The niches of the choir stalls contain sculptures by Louis-Philippe Hébert of the prophets, patriarchs, apostles, and evangelists. Father Bouillon was very proud of these stalls, which he probably modelled on those in Auch cathedral in France.

55

On 27 April 1865 he left Montreal for Santa Fe, New Mexico, after which, it appears, he went to Mexico City.[13] His biographers point out that he may have been invited there to teach drawing, along with several other French-speaking brothers, by Maximilian of Austria, who had been enthroned as emperor of Mexico by Napoleon III.[14]

Brother Gelasian would have been qualified for the Mexican mission by virtue of his talents in the graphic arts. He had very likely studied drawing in Montreal, as the Brothers' Institute developed technical

56

instruction very early to encourage careers in commerce and industry.[15] On the other hand, between 1860 and 1865 Montreal offered a number of opportunities to those interested in art and architecture. Napoléon Bourassa, architect and painter, had initiated courses in drawing at this time – at the Jacques-Cartier normal school, Sainte-Marie college, and the Société des artisans canadiens-français. The Mechanic Institute was also offering courses in technical and architectural drafting, and many painters, sculptors, and architects were advertising their services as teachers in the daily newspapers.[16]

Georges Bouillon's Mexican adventure was cut short. In 1866 the United States forced the French troops to withdraw from Mexico and supported the reinstatement of Republican President Benito Juárez; the French, along with other Francophone residents, beat a hasty retreat on the eve of Maximilian's execution. Brother Gelasian took refuge in Saint Louis, Missouri, where his community was active. Deeply affected by this brief but dramatic adventure, he was not content to return to Montreal as a teaching brother. On 5 June 1866 he left the Institute in Saint Louis and returned to Rimouski, where he completed his classical

Presbytery of the parish of Saint-François-de-Sales, Gatineau, designed by Georges Bouillon in 1879.

57

58

Presbytery of the parish of Saint-Benoît-Labre, Wendover, designed and built by Georges Bouillon in 1888.

studies at the college-seminary in 1866–67. He had in fact decided to become a priest, a move that would ease his ascent through the ranks of a religious hierarchy already well established in French Canada.[17]

Feeling somewhat confined in his native town, Georges Bouillon responded to an appeal from Monsignor J.-E. Bruno Guigues, Oblate Father and first bishop of Ottawa, for recruits to his order and his new diocese. In 1867, at the age of twenty-six, the young man from Rimouski made the move to Ottawa. He entered the University of Ottawa, which had just obtained its charter (1866), and taught drawing in the university's commercial course. In 1871 his talents as a drafts-man won him an invitation to prepare the plans for the new Notre Dame Cemetery, and the following year Father Joseph-Henri Tabaret, rector of the university, invited him to draw up plans for the interior of the Hull Church of Notre-Dame-de-Grâce.

Georges Bouillon remained for five years at this university, founded and managed by the Oblate Fathers, and one might assume that the ex-teaching brother would have considered joining the Oblate order.

However, this initially bilingual institution rapidly began to cut back on French-language instruction, for practical reasons,[18] which may have motivated Bouillon to complete his theological training at the Séminaire de Montréal. He enrolled there in October 1872 and, in a letter to Monsignor Guigues, thanked the bishop for having kindly agreed to defray his board and living expenses.[19]

The Diocesan Architect

The seminarian corresponded regularly with his patron. In October 1873 he informed him that he wished to obtain a post in the episcopal see, adding that his spiritual director did not feel him to be suited for a parish ministry and had advised him against entering a religious order.[20] In December 1873, worried by the bishop's uncertain health, he requested authorization to be ordained a priest, even though he had not finished the regulation time required by the seminary.[21] His request was granted, and Bouillon was ordained on 25 January 1874 by Monsignor Édouard-Charles Fabre, bishop of Montreal. The new priest had just enough time to return to Ottawa to attend the funeral of Monsignor Guigues, who died on 8 February.

Georges Bouillon quickly earned the confidence of the bishop's successor, Monsignor Joseph-Thomas Duhamel. In fact, in 1876, after only two years as an assistant curé, he became parish priest of the cathedral, the largest parish in the diocese, which he served until 1883. Father Bouillon was in charge of all work on the interior of the cathedral from 1878 to 1883, and demonstrated decided expertise, even though his furnishings and decor were much influenced by the interior of the Church of Notre Dame in Montreal, the work of architect Victor Bourgeau (1809–1888).

This first masterwork made Georges Bouillon known outside his parish, where his talent could find expression only in a few modest projects.[22] Thus, in 1879 "Messire George de Bouillon" produced the plans for the presbytery of Saint-François-de-Sales in Gatineau, a residence that stands today.[23]

In 1881 the parish priest of the cathedral sent a sketch "of the future cathedral of Buckingham" to the bishop, who was visiting Rome. Father Bouillon described it as "a Romano-Byzantine plan" and provided some dimensions, leaving it to the bishop "to decide what is appropriate in this matter."[24] The bishop considered the project too grandiose, and the architect set to work again. In 1882 he wrote that he had just completed a sketch for a new church, "very simple, with a single roof and a turret near the sacristy as Father Michel wishes . . . and two chapels by the choir as indicated in his plan."[25] From the outset of his architectural career, then, Georges Bouillon gave evidence of a propensity for the monumental and the grandiose, which was to be responsible for a number of the setbacks he would suffer.

In 1883, Bouillon saw the possibility of his becoming titular diocesan architect and convinced the bishop to find a replacement for him as parish priest of the cathedral. To acquire a general education in history and architecture, he immediately began a long journey through Europe and the Near East.

He left Ottawa at the end of summer of that year, going first to England, then to France. In Paris, in October, he announced his departure for Istanbul with stops at Strasbourg, Munich, Vienna, and Bucharest.[26] From Istanbul he travelled to Palestine, then to Malta and Italy. After visiting Pompeii and Naples, he arrived in Rome at the beginning of December. He set out again in February and toured northern Italy, southern France, Algeria, and Spain. In March 1884, in Paris, he announced that he would return to Ottawa for Easter.[27]

This overseas tour of about eight months enabled the architect-priest to become familiar with the great, historic buildings of Christianity. He was dazzled by three of these: Hagia Sophia in Istanbul, St. John's in Jerusalem, and St. Peter's in Rome. Of the latter, he said: "I have seen nothing grander and more sumptuous . . . it is certainly the finest and greatest of all Christian buildings."[28] His letters also testify to his aversion to the "infidel" Muslims, his enthusiasm for Spain "which deserves to be called 'Catholic' both for the grandeur of its religious buildings . . . and for the faith of its people," and a definite mistrust of "unhappy Italy" which had broken with the political tutelage of the Church. Finally, he said that he found "this great Paris" thoroughly detestable: he stayed there only to accept delivery of some furnishings he had commissioned for the cathedral in Ottawa.

After being named bursar of the diocese of Ottawa, Bouillon finally found the time to devote himself to architecture. From 1884 to 1888 he was very active in this field; at this time Monsignor Duhamel mentions him as being "his architect"[29] and the diocesan archives indicate that he was involved in a number of building projects. His most outstanding works date from this period, among them, the Church of Saint-François-de-Sales in Gatineau, the chapel of the Convent of Our Lady of the Sacred Heart in Ottawa, the chapel of the University of Ottawa, and the Church of Notre-Dame-de-Lourdes in Vanier (formerly Eastview).

However, this period in his career, as when he had served with the Brothers of Christian Schools, was very short. In 1889, Father Bouillon was appointed canon of the cathedral, an honorary title that compensated somewhat for his having been bypassed as diocesan architect.

Church of Saint-François-de-Sales, Gatineau. The nave and façade were designed by Georges Bouillon in 1886 and built in 1886–87.

59

Nevertheless, he retained his duties as bursar of the diocese (created an archdiocese in 1886) and was also named secretary to Monsignor Duhamel.

There is no precise indication of why the canon stopped practising architecture in the archdiocese of Ottawa. But as he tried to continue working elsewhere, it may be assumed that the diocesan authorities were turning to other architects, probably because of certain problems that had arisen on Bouillon's work sites and the lack of unanimity about the nature of his work. For example, we know that construction dragged on the Church of Notre-Dame-de-Lourdes, and that the plans

60

In 1901, Georges Bouillon designed the interior decor of the Church of Saint-François-de-Sales, Gatineau, including this pulpit, altarpiece, and fan vaulting, as they appeared in a photograph of about 1930.

Bouillon submitted for the new church in Mattawa were rejected in 1888. A year earlier, Monsignor Duhamel had called on the services of Father Joseph Michaud,[30] architect-priest of the diocese of Montreal, to whom he had turned in the past when Bouillon was fully occupied by his pastoral duties;[31] it was Michaud who had produced the plans for the Ottawa Church of Saint-Jean-Baptiste in 1881. Some time later, Montreal architect Louis-Zéphirin Gauthier became Monsignor Duhamel's protégé, and remained so until 1902.[32]

From all this we may conclude that Georges Bouillon met with little success in architecture when he was required to define an overall

The choir of the Church of Notre-Dame-de-Lourdes, Vanier (Eastview), designed by Georges Bouillon in 1886. The church was destroyed by fire in 1973.

61

CHAPTER IV

project and to produce an estimate and a timetable. On the other hand, his "artistic talent" was recognized, and it was this that enabled him to continue designing interiors.

A Career in Quebec?

In June 1888, Canon Bouillon undertook a second European tour. He visited London, "which is becoming more and more beautiful," and noted once again that "if Paris is the paradise of the French ... most of them will have no other." This time his travels also took him to Lyons, Rome, and points in Austria.[33] On his return to Ottawa, he carried out his duties at the episcopal palace without involving himself much in architecture. He was content to supervise the final work on the cathedral's interior decor though, somewhat grumpily, he would occasionally vent an acrid comment on the buildings being erected in the archdiocese.[34] In May 1891 he left for Europe again, and on 4 June wrote to his bishop: "It seems to me that my mission in Ottawa is finished." In the same breath, he requested authorization to retire as a monk with the Carthusians of St. Hugh's Parkminster in Sussex, England.[35] Monsignor Duhamel agreed to this request, but Bouillon remained in the abbey for only four months. In October 1891, finding the life of a recluse intolerable, he begged his patron to allow him to return to Ottawa.[36]

No sooner back in Ottawa, and probably dissatisfied with his responsibilities in the archdiocese – the same as he had had before his departure – Bouillon tried to redirect his career. In 1892 he was deeply affected by the death of his father. No longer feeling useful in Ottawa, he went to Haverhill, Massachusetts, where he assisted a sick colleague in a parish ministry. Then he visited his sister and three nieces in Fall River. Moved by the chronic poverty of his family, he beseeched his bishop to assign him a pastoral post in a well-to-do parish so that he could help them out, but his entreaties went unanswered.[37]

However, these excursions enabled Georges Bouillon to turn himself to account as an architect outside Ottawa, thanks especially to his reputation as the architect responsible for the interior decor of the cathedral. His first major project was the chapel of the Collège de Lévis, the plans for which he produced in 1891. Construction was delayed for financial reasons and the building was not completed until 1900, to the plans of Quebec City architects Peachy and Dussault. This first project by the architect-priest outside his own diocese set the tone for those to follow. Recognized for his ability to rework the formal vocabulary of religious buildings, and appreciated in Quebec where rich, exuberant interiors suited the taste of a new, moneyed, rural middle class, Georges Bouillon became an adviser to many priests and bishops, former colleagues or at least men of his own generation. But with the formation

Members of the Venerable Chapter of the Basilica of Ottawa, 9 October, 1889. Front row, from the left: Very Reverend Georges Bouillon, Monsignor J.O. Routhier, Monsignor Joseph-Thomas Duhamel (archbishop of Ottawa), Very Reverend L.N. Campeau, Very Reverend J.A. Plantin. Back row, from the left: Very Reverend P. McCarthy, Very Reverend D.F. Foley, Very Reverend S. Philip, Very Reverend F. Michel, Very Reverend P. Bélanger.

of the Province of Quebec Association of Architects in 1890 and the adoption of the first regulations governing the profession, he was excluded from practising as an architect. From that point on, Bouillon's plans would outline only the concept of a project; the actual construction would be the responsibility of a lay architect, translating into realistic terms the often overly grandiose ideas of the canon.

In 1893 Georges Bouillon was invited to finish the interior decor of the Rimouski cathedral. As in Ottawa, this was a structure built to the plans of Victor Bourgeau. However, Bouillon's project, which

The interior of the Cathedral
of Rimouski, designed by Georges
Bouillon and destroyed during
renovations in the 1970s. The
baldachin, that preeminently
baroque ornamental structure over
the altar, is here transposed into
the Gothic vocabulary by the
architect.

63

64

Convent of the Sisters of Notre-
Dame du Saint Rosaire, Rimouski,
as seen about 1920. Construction
began in 1904 to a design by
Georges Bouillon of 1898. The
building exists today but has been
modified.

The archbishop's residence in Rimouski, built between 1901 and 1903 to George Bouillon's original design (1898), and reworked by architect Joseph J.-B. Verret.

65

The Church of Sainte-Cécile, parish of Bic, built in 1891–92 by architect Pierre Lévesque.

66

included expanding the choir as well as creating furnishings and a painted interior decor, was deferred. After consulting with the architect Napoléon Bourassa, the bishop, Monsignor Albert Blais, retained the services of Joseph J.-B. Verret, a Sherbrooke architect, enjoining him to take his inspiration from Canon Bouillon's drafts. As a result, Bouillon's contribution was confined to the cathedral's interior, and Verret was entrusted with supervising the work.

Although the bishop of Rimouski's confidence in the canon was evidently limited, Bouillon's reputation as an artist and an innovator earned him a few more assignments in the region. In 1898 he drafted plans for a convent for the Sisters of Notre-Dame du Saint Rosaire in Rimouski and designed interiors for the churches in Bic and Trois-Pistoles. But here, too, the final plans were approved by licensed architects.

Increasingly absent from Ottawa, Canon Bouillon was named assistant to the parish priest of the cathedral in 1896. The following year he obtained (as compensation, one might suppose) the title of "chanoine primicier" (senior member of the board) of the metropolitan (Ottawa) chapter of the province.

Plan of the choir baldachin, Church of Sainte-Cécile, parish of Bic, designed by Georges Bouillon in 1898. The decor was installed in 1899–1900.

He nonetheless obtained the commission to prepare construction plans for the new Dominican monastery beside the Church of Saint-Jean-Baptiste in Ottawa. In 1897 he went to Rome to defend his proposal, and two years later work began.[38] Through repeated trips to Massachusetts he also spread his influence there. In 1902 he proposed a decor for the Church of Our Lady of Lourdes in Fall River and was asked to oversee its execution. He also drafted quite elaborate plans for the Church of St. Anthony in Manchester, New Hampshire. Two years later, he was back in Ottawa to submit plans for the interior decor of the Church of Saint-Paul in Aylmer.

The Last Dreams
In 1904 Georges Bouillon left the Ottawa see for the last time. He was named chaplain of St. Joseph's Orphanage in the city and priest in

Engraving after a drawing by Georges Bouillon, dated 1898, of the "Monastery of the Reverend Dominican Fathers in Ottawa." Bouillon planned to erect a new façade in front of the Church of Saint-Jean-Baptiste, erected in 1882–83 to the plans of Father Joseph Michaud. He then proposed a building, to the left, for the friars. Work began in 1899 but was never completed. The whole complex was destroyed by fire in 1931.

68

charge of the hospice of St. Charles. Until 1910, he lived with his sister in a house that he owned at 178 Rideau Terrace. Most of his drawings, which might be described as "dreams of an architect," date from this period. They are preserved today in the Archives nationales du Québec in Trois-Rivières.

Starting in 1902, Bouillon had determined on a grand project, the culmination of his life's work – a *Nova Sancta Sophia.* Initially planned for New York, this imposing basilica sought a site for many years, and he was constantly drafting detailed plans and elevations until 1911. The cartons of Bouillon's papers in the archives also contain plans for a church called Notre-Dame-de-la-Paix, "of the same size as Sancta Sophia," and a proposal for a new provincial museum that from 1908 was considered for the Plains of Abraham in Quebec City. Probably

Drawing by Georges Bouillon, dated 1904, of the choir screen for the Church of Saint-Paul in Aylmer, part of a reconstruction project for the Aylmer church which had been destroyed by fire that year.

69

96

because he had found it an interesting experience to serve as a jury member in 1896 for the competition to select the best design for the Champlain monument in Quebec City,[39] Bouillon registered in 1907 for the open competition to prepare plans for government office buildings and a Department of Justice building in Ottawa. This incursion into the realm of civil architecture ended in resounding defeat: Georges Bouillon finished twenty-sixth, receiving 35 points out of 100. The verdict by architect Edmund Burke, a member of the examining committee, was

Nova Sancta Sophia. Plan by Georges Bouillon, dated about 1902, envisioned for many sites, including New York City, but never realized.

Floor plan of the museum proposed by Georges Bouillon about 1908 for the Plains of Abraham in Quebec City.

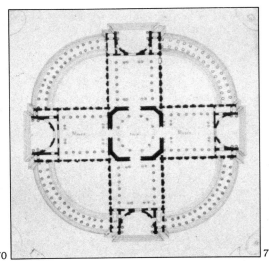

70

71

CHAPTER IV

harsh: "This plan is not an architectural creation and is entirely unsuitable for the purposes for which it is intended and is entirely out of harmony with the existing buildings."[40] Indeed, the old architect had not realized that a good many things had changed since the turn of the century; of this he was being brutally reminded.

Retiring to the St. Charles hospice in 1911, Bouillon obtained authorization in 1912 to return to live in the archbishop's palace. Two years later he accepted the post of chaplain with the Sister Adorers of the Precious Blood. In 1923 he withdrew to join the Dominicans of Notre-Dame-de-Grâce in Montreal. There, in 1925 at the age of eighty-four, he learned that the pope had elevated him to the rank of Domestic Prelate. When in 1931 his bishop forbade him to celebrate mass because of his advanced age, he returned to Ottawa, where he died on 6 April 1932 at the age of ninety-one.

An impressive figure, tall of stature and elegant, Georges Bouillon was a true prince of the Church. However, his health was fragile, he had little self-confidence, and he was somewhat arrogant and unstable, ceaselessly redirecting his career and complaining about his lot, always in search of an elusive perfection. He proved to be much more an artist than a leader of men, and he had more need of others than the capacity to help them. Nevertheless, when encouraged by his superiors and supported by the climate of his time, he succeeded in creating a number of lasting and distinctive works, while at the same time bearing witness to the hope and faith that inspired the members of the Canadian Church in the second half of the nineteenth century.

Perspective of a plan submitted by Georges Bouillon to a competition in 1907 for a new government building facing Major's Hill Park in Ottawa.

GEORGES BOUILLON, ARCHITECT

A still-life watercolour inscribed: *Je n'aurai sur mon tombeau ni fleur ni pierre,/Souvenez-vous de moi dans une fervente prière* ("Neither flower nor stone will I have on my grave/ Remember me simply in an ardent prayer"). The picture is signed Canon G. Bouillon and dated 19 November 1920.

73

NOTES AND REFERENCES

I THE CHAPEL WITHIN THE MUSEUM

1. Annual Report 1972–1973, Heritage Committee, A Capital for Canadians, Ottawa, 1973.
2. Letter of 9 March 1971 from R.A.J. Phillips to Mother Marcelle Gauthier, Superior General of the Sisters of Charity; file of the Convent of Our Lady of the Sacred Heart, archives of the National Capital Commission.
3. R.A.J. Phillips, "Anatomy of a Struggle," Annual Report 1972–1973, Heritage Committee, A Capital for Canadians, Ottawa, 1973.
4. "Don't wreck it," letter from R.A.J. Phillips in *The Ottawa Citizen*, 26 March 1971, p. 6.
5. *The Ottawa Journal*, 17 May 1971.
6. *The Ottawa Citizen*, 14 December 1971.
7. *The Ottawa Citizen*, 21 January 1972. See also Michael Newton, "National Capital Commission: Participation in the Salvaging of the Rideau Street Convent Chapel, 1970–88," National Capital Commission, April 1988.
8. Report by Hazen Sise, 7 April 1972; file of the Convent of Our Lady of the Sacred Heart, archives of the National Capital Commission.
9. *The Ottawa Citizen*, 21 April 1972.
10. Letter of 26 April 1972 from the Hon. Jean Chrétien, Minister of Indian Affairs and Northern Development, to the National Capital Commission, archives of the National Capital Commission.
11. *The Ottawa Citizen*, 29 April 1972.
12. Ibid.
13. *The Ottawa Citizen*, 6 May 1972.
14. *The Ottawa Journal*, 12 May 1972.
15. "Convent in distress, photogrammetry to the rescue," *Science Dimension*, IV:4, August 1972, pp. 1–7.
16. *Le Droit*, 4 February 1974.
17. "The Cloisters," *The Metropolitan Museum of Art Bulletin*, XXXVII:1, Summer 1979.
18. "Drawing Room for Landsdowne House," *Bulletin, Philadelphia Museum of Art*, LXXXII:351–52, Summer 1986.
19. Harold Kalman et al, *The Rideau Street Convent Chapel: Restoration Methods and Their Implications*, research report prepared for the National Gallery of Canada (Ottawa: Commonwealth Historic Resource Management Limited, 15 August 1984).
20. See note 13, chapter II.
21. On the stages of the installation of the interior decor, see Harold Kalman et al, *Rideau Street Convent Chapel: Preparation for Installation* (Ottawa: Commonwealth Historic Resource Management Limited, March 1987). See also Harold Kalman, "Restoration of the Chapel of the Rideau Street Convent," *The Journal of the Association for Preservation Technology*, VIII:4, 1986, pp. 18–29.

II A MASTERWORK ON DISPLAY

1. There are at present no studies on the evolution of the church and the chapel as architectural types in Quebec and in Canada.

However, some key features of religious architecture may be found in Luc Noppen, *Les églises du Québec* (Montreal: Fides, 1977), 298 pp.

2. The last big outer chapels were built about 1850. See Robert Caron, *Un couvent du XIXᵉ siècle: La maison des Soeurs de la Charité de Québec* (Montreal: Libre Expression, 1980), 148 pp.

3. Luc Noppen, op. cit., pp. 188–89.

4. "As for the layout of the premises, the chapel occupied the room now used as a classroom for young French-Canadian girls, second floor, corner of Waller and Rideau Streets." Chroniques du pensionnat Notre-Dame-du-Sacré-Coeur, Vol. I, folio iii, 1869, archives of the Sisters of Charity, Ottawa.

5. Chroniques de la maison mère, Vol. I, 3 November 1882, archives of the Sisters of Charity, Ottawa.

6. Chroniques du pensionnat Notre-Dame-du-Sacré-Coeur, Vol. I, 1887, p. 70, archives of the Sisters of Charity, Ottawa.

7. Walter C. Leedy, *Fan Vaulting: A Study of Form, Technology and Meaning* (Santa Monica: Arts and Architecture Press, 1980), p. 1.

8. He wrote, for example, on 3 January 1881, "Buckingham is big enough to have a church that redounds to the credit of Catholicism in that den of Orangemen."; Georges Bouillon file, archives of the archdiocese of Ottawa.

9. Letter of 12 July 1888 from Father Augier, provincial, Mattawa file, archives of the province, Oblates of Mary Immaculate, Montreal.

10. *Le Canada*, Ottawa, 26 June 1888, p. 1.

11. See note 1, chapter III.

12. For example, Tewkesbury Abbey; St. George's Chapel, Windsor; Lady Chapel, Canterbury Cathedral; Bath Abbey; Peterborough Cathedral; Ramryge Chapel, St. Alban's Cathedral; and St. Stephen's Cloister in the Houses of Parliament at Westminster.

13. For example: Frederick Mackenzie, *Observations on the Construction of the Roof of King's College Chapel, Cambridge* (London: John Weale, 1840); John Britton and E.W. Brayley, *The History of the Ancient Palace and Late Houses of Parliament at Westminster* (London: John Weale, 1836); L.N. Cottingham, *Plans, Elevations, Section and Details of Henry VII's Chapel, Westminster*, 2 vols. (London, 1822–29).

14. "Mémoire de M. Willis sur la construction des voûtes au Moyen-Âge, traduit de l'anglais par M. César Daly," *Revue Générale de l'Architecture et des Travaux Publics*, Vol. IV, 1843, pp. 3–14, 289–304, 481–507. Translated from R. Willis, "On the Construction of the Vaults of the Middle Ages," *Transactions of the Royal Institute of British Architects*, Vol. I, part 2, 1842, p. 43.

15. "Mémoire de M. Willis sur la construction des voûtes au Moyen-Âge, traduit de l'anglais par M. César Daly," op. cit., p. 502.

16. In medieval naves with no side aisles, fan vaults were built on square bays. When the building possessed side aisles, a different vaulting technique was used.

17. "Mémoire de M. Willis sur la construction des voûtes au Moyen-Âge, traduit de l'anglais par M. César Daly," op. cit., p. 491.

18. In 1790–92, in St. George's Chapel, Windsor, the architect Henry Emlyn assembled the vault under the balcony with modular elements in plaster. See Alison Kelly, "Coade Stone in Georgian Architecture," *Architectural History: Journal of the Society of Architectural Historians of Great Britain*, XXVIII, 1985, illus. p. 99.

19. Illustrated in James Macaulay, *The Gothic Revival, 1745–1845* (London: Blackie, 1975), p. 147.

20. Illustrated in Henry-Russell Hitchcock, *Architecture: Nineteenth and Twentieth Centuries* (Harmondsworth: Penguin Books, 1958), pl. 60 B.

21. James Macaulay, op. cit., pp. 265–66.

22. It should also be pointed out that, according to the plans of the architect James O'Donnell (1825), the vault of the Church of Notre Dame in Montreal would seem to have some affinity with a fan vault. See Franklin K.B.S. Toker, *The Church of Notre Dame in Montreal: An Architectural History* (Montreal and London: McGill-Queen's University Press, 1970), pl. 18, 19.

23. The decor by Victor Bourgeau for the choir of the Church of Notre Dame in Montreal, dating from 1876, only developed James O'Donnell's work.

24. Claudette Lacelle, "Conefroy, Pierre," *Dictionary of Canadian Biography*, Vol. V, pp. 202–203; Luc Noppen, *Notre-Dame de Québec: Son architecture, son rayonnement (1647–1922)* (Quebec City: Éditions du Pélican, 1974), pp. 160–61.

25. Luc Noppen and Marc Grignon, *L'art de l'architecte: Trois siècles de dessin d'architecture à Québec* (Quebec City: Musée du Québec, 1983), pp. 76–81.

26. Ultramontanism is a doctrine advocating absolute papal authority and the primacy of the Roman Catholic Church. Monsignor Ignace Bourget, bishop of Montreal from 1840 to 1876, was its most famous proponent in Quebec.

27. Georges-Émile Giguère, "Martin, Félix," *Dictionary of Canadian Biography*, Vol. XI, pp. 587–89.

28. Father Joseph Michaud file, Gérard Morisset collection, Inventaire des biens culturels, Ministère des Affaires culturelles, Province de Québec.

29. Monsignor Duhamel's correspondence mentions this architect's name several times. See, for example, letters of 7 October 1880 and 18 November 1887, correspondence of Monsignor Duhamel, archives of the archdiocese of Ottawa.

30. Jacques Robert, "Jean-Thomas Nadeau et l'élaboration d'une théorie architecturale au Québec (1914–1934)," Master's thesis (Quebec City: Laval University, 1980), 173 pp.

31. Nicole Tardif-Painchaud, *Dom Bellot et l'architecture religieuse au Québec* (Quebec City: Laval University Press, 1978), p. 262.

32. Raymond Vézina, "L'influence du sentiment religieux sur l'art," *Napoléon Bourassa (1827–1916): Introduction à l'étude de son art* (Montreal: Éditions Élysée, 1976), pp. 173–86.

33. Raymond Vézina, op. cit., pp. 146, 148, 150.

34. Letter of 31 January 1882, Georges Bouillon file, archives of the archdiocese of Ottawa.

35. Ibid., letter of 23 October 1883.

36. César Daly, "De l'Architecture de l'Avenir: À propos de la Renaissance française, un chapitre de philosophie d'histoire générale et d'art," *Revue Générale de l'Architecture et des Travaux Publics*, 1856, p. 19ff.

37. Ibid., p. 68.

38. Ibid., p. 70.
39. Letter of 27 January 1879, Georges Bouillon file, archives of the archdiocese of Ottawa.
40. Letter from the architect Joseph J.-B. Verret of 2 May 1901, correspondence of Monsignor Blais, archives of the diocese of Rimouski.

III THE BIRTH OF A CHAPEL

1. The most complete document on the history of the convent and the chapel is by Harold Kalman et al, *The Rideau Street Convent Chapel: A History*, research report prepared for the National Gallery of Canada (Ottawa: Commonwealth Historic Resource Management Limited, 1984), 67 pp. The most detailed document on the convent alone is the report by Marsha Snizer and Marc Lafrance, *Rideau Street Convent* (Ottawa: Parks Canada, May 1972), 4 pp.
2. P. Alexis [de Barbezieux], *Histoire de la Province Ecclésiastique d'Ottawa*, Vol. I (Ottawa, 1897), p. 294.
3. Minutes of the general council, Vol. G3-1A2, p. 332, meeting of 20 May 1869, archives of the Sisters of Charity, Ottawa.
4. Ibid., p. 333, meeting of 2 June 1869. The price paid was $14,125.
5. *Le Canada*, Ottawa, 19 June 1869.
6. Harold Kalman and John Roaf, *Exploring Ottawa* (Toronto: University of Toronto Press, 1983), pp. 62–63.
7. The building bought by the nuns was in fact constructed at two different times. The eastern section, with its façade on Rideau Street, seemed older and more carefully executed, with a ground floor in bossage stone and a carriage gateway. It was also more like a house, with access to the upper storeys by a staircase at the left rear, and a store on the ground floor, indicated by a central door framed by two shop windows. The building on the corner was probably the section built about 1855 by a certain McIntosh for the hotel owner Thomas Mathews; see Marsha Snizer and Marc Lafrance, op. cit., p. 2. The name "Revere House" was later adopted by another inn on Sussex Street; see Harold Kalman, op. cit., p. 30.
8. Minutes of the general council, Vol. G3-1A2, p. 377, meeting of 29 December 1871; ibid., p. 378, meeting of 8 January 1872; Vol. GA-1A3, p. 41, meeting of 5 December 1872; archives of the Sisters of Charity, Ottawa.
9. Ibid., Vol. G3-1A3, p. 182, meeting of 2 May 1880.
10. Ibid., p. 315, meeting of 2 May 1886.
11. Ibid., p. 337, meeting of 8 January 1887.
12. Ibid., pp. 453–54, meeting of 23 December 1892.
13. Chroniques du pensionnat Notre-Dame-du-Sacré-Coeur, 1869–1908, March 1887, p. 70, archives of the Sisters of Charity, Ottawa.
14. Ibid.
15. Ibid., "For some days now workers have been busy surrounding us with a wall of stones, which means that work on the chapel will definitely begin in the spring."
16. Ibid., 23 April 1887, p. 71.
17. Ibid., 19 February 1888, p. 81.
18. The costs changed rapidly and substantially. On 2 March 1887 *Le Canada* reported that the cost of the new building would be $10,000; the *Evening Journal* of 25 June 1888 mentioned the sum of $23,000; and the Grey Nuns' chronicles of 22 May 1888 noted that they had estimated the total cost at over $40,000.
19. Chroniques du pensionnat Notre-Dame-du-Sacré-Coeur, 23 April 1887, pp. 70–71, archives of the Sisters of Charity, Ottawa.
20. Ibid., 25 June 1888, p. 85.
21. *Evening Journal*, 25 June 1888, p. 1; *Le Canada*, 26 June 1888, no. 368, p. 1; *Daily Citizen*, 26 June 1888, p. 3.
22. *Free Press*, 25 June 1888.
23. Minutes of the general council, Vol. 9, p. 121, meeting of 22 November 1926; ibid., p. 122, meeting of 15 January 1927; ibid., p. 124, meeting of 21 January 1927; ibid., pp. 126–27, meeting of 10 March 1927; archives of the Sisters of Charity, Ottawa. Werner Noffke was the architect of this block.
24. "The Superior of the Rideau Street Boarding School has requested authorization to add one storey and to have the roof of her institution raised; this has been granted." Minutes of the general council, Vol. G3-1A4, p. 17, meeting of 2 February 1899; archives of the Sisters of Charity, Ottawa.
25. "The Rideau Street façade has received a substantial extension with the restrained, classic lines of the original building. On the ground floor, the vast red parlour, in the English style, is a counterpart to the green parlour, the former lounge of the Mathews Hotel and the institution's chapel until 1887. On the first floor, a library, in the Ruskin style, has become a favourite retreat of the alumnae, who have completely furnished it. The upper floors are for private rooms and dormitories for the younger boarders."; see Sister Paul-Émile and Hector Legros, *Le diocèse d'Ottawa 1847–1948* (Ottawa: Le Droit, 1949) pp. 581–82.
26. Minutes of the general council, Vol. G3-1A4, p. 105, meeting of 2 July 1904, archives of the Sisters of Charity, Ottawa.
27. Ibid., p. 459, meeting of 15 October 1920.
28. See note 23.
29. For Jean-Serge Le Fort's gymnasium plans, see archives of the Sisters of Charity, Ottawa, June 1964.

IV GEORGES BOUILLON, ARCHITECT

1. Anson A. Gard, *The Hub and the Spokes, or the Capital and Its Environs* (Ottawa: Emerson Press, 1904), pp. 137–38.
2. *Le Droit*, Thursday, 7 April 1932. On Saturday, 9 April, under the headline, "Impressive funeral service for Mgr. Bouillon," the same newspaper listed about a hundred dignitaries, friends, and relations attending the service that morning.
3. For example, *Le Devoir* and *The Ottawa Citizen*, 8 April 1932, and the *Bulletin de l'Amicale du Séminaire de Rimouski*, 24, 1 May 1932, p. 60.
4. The official biography provided by the archdiocese of Ottawa, which was reproduced in *Le Droit*'s April 7 number, can be found in J.-B.-A. Allaire, *Dictionnaire biographique du clergé*

canadien-français, Vol. VI (Saint-Hyacinthe: Le Courrier, 1934), pp. 129–30.

5. Gérard Morisset, *L'architecture en Nouvelle-France* (Quebec City, 1949), p. 126.

6. Marion MacRae and Anthony Adamson, *Hallowed Walls: Church Architecture of Upper Canada* (Toronto: Clarke, Irwin & Co., 1975), p. 247.

7. P. Alexis [de Barbezieux], *Histoire de la Province Ecclésiastique d'Ottawa*, Vol. II (Ottawa, 1897), p. 24.

8. The cathedral account books, 1877–94, archives of the archdiocese of Ottawa.

9. "On February eleventh, one thousand eight hundred forty-one, we the undersigned, curate of this parish, baptized George, born the same day of the legitimate marriage of George Bouillon, farmer of this place, and Marie des Anges Lavoie . . . "; archives of the parish of Saint-Germain in Rimouski, Register of Births, Deaths, and Marriages, 11 February 1841.

10. Nive Voisine, *Les Frères des Écoles chrétiennes au Canada* (Quebec City: Éditions Anne Sigier, 1987), pp 47–71.

11. This was the name popularly given to the brothers at this time.

12. Georges Bouillon file, archives of the Brothers of Christian Schools, Sainte-Dorothée.

13. Ibid.

14. "In 1865, Emperor Maximilian of Mexico wrote to Pope Pius IX asking for a teacher of drawing and calligraphy for the Brothers' Mexican schools. The Superior General of the Brothers of Christian Schools appointed Brother Bouillon on the instruction of His Holiness, and in this capacity he spent one year in Mexico."; "Feu Mgr Bouillon," *Bulletin de l'Amicale du Séminaire de Rimouski*, XXIV, 1 May 1932, p. 60.

15. For example, Brothers Stanislas and Arnold, native Frenchmen, taught drawing at the École Sainte-Anne; see Georges Rigault, *Histoire des Frères des Écoles Chrétiennes*, Vol. IX, p. 30ff.

16. Raymond Vézina, *Napoléon Bourassa (1827–1916): Introduction à l'étude de son art* (Montreal: Éditions Élysée, 1976), pp. 26–27.

17. It should be pointed out that the Brothers of Christian Schools seemed to reserve their key positions for Frenchmen from France, and that, at least until 1860–65, the French-Canadians in the group, who were moreover required to take an English name to distinguish them from the European French, were apparently no match for the English-speaking group formed by the native Irish.

18. Gaston Carrière, "Tabaret, Joseph-Henri," *Dictionary of Canadian Biography*, Vol. XI, pp. 867–68.

19. Letter of 17 October 1872, Georges Bouillon file, archives of the archdiocese of Ottawa.

20. Ibid., letter of 18 October 1873.

21. Ibid., letter of 27 December 1873. The required period was three and one-half years.

22. In 1879, Georges Bouillon carried out some repairs to certain diocesan properties, including the chapel of Notre Dame Cemetery and lodges for the caretaker and gardener; letter of 15 July 1879, Georges Bouillon file, archives of the archdiocese of Ottawa.

23. "Approval of construction of a new presbytery, which will cost about two thousand five hundred dollars according to the estimates of 'the Reverend Messire George de Bouillon,' who has prepared the plan . . ."; Minutes (1872–1912), p. 18, meeting of 26 October 1879, archives of the parish of Saint-François-de-Sales, Gatineau.

24. Letter of 3 January 1881, Georges Bouillon file, archives of the archdiocese of Ottawa.

25. Ibid., letter of 20 February 1882.

26. Ibid., letter of 5 October 1883.

27. Ibid., letters of 23 October and 5 December 1883, and 12 March 1884.

28. Ibid., letter of 5 December 1883.

29. Letter of 3 May 1887, correspondence of Monsignor Duhamel, archives of the archdiocese of Ottawa.

30. Ibid., letter of 18 November 1887.

31. Ibid., letter of 7 October 1880.

32. Ibid., letter of 22 August 1899.

33. Letter of 15 July 1888, Georges Bouillon file, archives of the archdiocese of Ottawa.

34. Ibid., letter of 8 December 1890.

35. Ibid., letter of 4 June 1891.

36. Ibid., letter of 27 October 1891.

37. Letters of 8 January 1892 and 27 May 1892, Georges Bouillon file; letter of 28 June 1892, correspondence of Monsignor Duhamel; archives of the archdiocese of Ottawa.

38. Letters of 22 October and 28 November 1897, Dominican file, archives of the archdiocese of Ottawa.

39. Letter of 24 February 1896, Georges Bouillon file, archives of the archdiocese of Ottawa.

40. *Construction*, October 1907, pp. 48–50; Robert G. Hill, "Horwood Papers," *The Biographical Dictionary of Architects in Canada, 1800–1930* (forthcoming).

CATALOGUE OF THE ARCHITECTURAL WORK
OF GEORGES BOUILLON

1871	Ottawa	Plan of Notre Dame Cemetery[1]	Completed in 1872
1872	Hull	Plans for the interior decor of the Church of Notre-Dame-de-Grâce[2]	Church built in 1870–71 and destroyed by fire in 1888
1876 to 1882	Ottawa	Interior decor of the Cathedral of Notre Dame[3]	Galleries, 1876; vaults and columns, 1878; side aisles, 1880; sanctuary, stalls, and high altar, 1881–83; extant
1877	Ottawa	Plan for the tomb of Mgr. Guigues in the cathedral crypt[4]	Built in 1877–78
1879	Gatineau	Plans for the presbytery of the parish of Saint-François-de-Sales[5]	Built in 1880–81; extant
1881	Buckingham	Plans for the Church of Saint-Grégoire[6]	Built in 1887–90; destroyed by fire in 1904
1881	Ottawa	Plans for the building and decor of the chapel of the mother house, Sisters of Charity, Sussex and Bruyère Streets[7]	Built from 1882 to 1885; extant but much changed by renovation during the 1960s
1881	Papineauville	Plans for the presbytery of the parish of Sainte-Angélique[8]	Built in 1882; extant

1884	Almonte	Plans for the cemetery[9]	Opened in August 1884
1884	Luskville	Plan for the Church of Saint-Dominique[10]	Built in 1884–85; extant
1885	Ottawa	Plans for interior decor of the Church of Saint-Jean-Baptiste, built in 1882–83, probably to the plans of Father Joseph Michaud[11]	Carried out in 1885–86; destroyed by fire in 1931
1885	Bonfield (Lac Talon, Callander)	Proposal for a church[12]	Not carried out
1885	Kanata (South March)	Plans for the Church of St. Isidore[13]	Built in 1887–88; extant
1886	Sarsfield	Plans for the presbytery of the parish of Saint-Hugues[14]	Built in 1887–88; extant
1886	Gatineau	Church of Saint-François-de-Sales; plans for the nave and façade to be added to choir and transept of 1873[15]	Built in 1886–87; extant
1886	Vanier (Eastview, Ottawa)	Plans for the Church of Notre-Dame-de-Lourdes[16]	Built in 1887–88; left unfinished; completed by two bays and a new façade in 1913; destroyed by fire in 1973
1886	Gower Point (La Passe)	Plans for the Church of Notre-Dame-du-Mont-Carmel[17]	Built in 1887–88
1887	Ottawa	Redevelopment plan for a building for the Sister Adorers of the Precious Blood of Saint-Hyacinthe[18]	Work completed in 1887; building replaced by another, to the plans of architect L.-Z. Gauthier, about 1895
1887	Ottawa	Plans for construction and decor of the chapel of the Convent of Our Lady of the Sacred Heart (Rideau Street Convent), Besserer and Waller Streets[19]	Chapel built in 1887–88; demolished in 1972; interior decor saved, in storage until 1986; installed in new building of the National Gallery of Canada in 1987–88
1887	Ottawa	Plans for interior decor of the chapel of the University of Ottawa[20]	Destroyed by fire in 1903
1888	Mattawa	Proposal for a church for the parish of Sainte-Anne[21]	Rejected; church built in 1888–89 to the plans of the architect Lauzon from Île Bizard; destroyed by fire in 1959

1888	Wendover	Plans for the presbytery of the parish of Saint-Benoît-Labre[22]	Completed in 1888
1891	Lévis	Plan for the chapel of the Collège de Lévis[23]	Building completed in 1900 under the supervision of architects Peachy and Dussault; extant
1893	Mattawa	Plans for the interior decor of the Church of Sainte-Anne[24]	Work completed in 1894; destroyed by fire in 1959
1893	Rimouski	Plans to enlarge the cathedral and plans for its interior decor[25]	Project abandoned, then resumed in 1898; carried out in 1902–03 to the plans as corrected by Joseph J.-B. Verret, Sherbrooke architect; interior decor destroyed about 1970
1898	Bic	Plans for the interior decor of the Church of Sainte-Cécile[26]	Decor installed in 1899–1900 in the church built in 1891–92 to the plans of architect Pierre Lévesque
1898	Ottawa	Plans for the Dominican convent and the redecoration of the façade of the Church of Saint-Jean-Baptiste[27]	Work begun in 1899; never entirely completed; complex destroyed by fire in 1931
1898	Rimouski	Plans for the bishop's (today the archbishop's) residence[28]	Built in 1901–1903 to plans corrected by Sherbrooke architect Joseph J.-B. Verret
1898	Rimouski	Plans for the convent of Notre-Dame du Saint Rosaire[29]	Construction from 1904; extant, but modified
1898	Trois-Pistoles	Plan for the interior decor of the Church of Notre-Dame-des-Neiges[30]	Carried out starting in 1902 under the direction of architect J. Joseph Pierre Ouellet
1901	Gatineau	Plans for the interior decor of the Church of Saint-François-de-Sales and the new sacristy[31]	Carried out in 1902–1903; renovated; partially extant
1902	Fall River (Mass.)	Plans for the interior decor and altar for the Church of Our Lady of Lourdes[32]	Carried out starting in 1902; extant
1902	No site	Project for a church: *Nova Sancta Sophia*[33]	Not carried out
1903	Rimouski	Plan for the altar of a private chapel in the bishop's residence[34]	Completed in 1903

1904	Aylmer	Plans for reconstruction of the Church of Saint-Paul and plans for interior decor[35]	Built in 1893–94 by Gauthier and Roy, architects; destroyed by fire in 1904 and rebuilt to original design in 1905–1908
c.1904	Ottawa (New Edinburgh)	Survey plan for a house, probably at 178 Rideau Terrace[36]	Building extant in 1904 (?); not standing today
1907	Ottawa	Submissions to a federal government building competition[37] (Department of Justice and office buildings)	Not carried out
c.1908	Quebec City	Proposal for the Musée du Québec[38]	Not carried out
1914	Saint-Moïse	Plans for the church[39]	Building extant
n.d.	Manchester (New Hampshire)	Proposal for a church[40]	Not carried out

1. P. Alexis [de Barbezieux], *Histoire de la Province Ecclésiastique d'Ottawa*, Vol. I (Ottawa, 1897), p. 495.
2. Gaston Carrière, *Histoire documentaire des Oblats de Marie-Immaculée,* Vol. VII (Ottawa: University of Ottawa Press, 1957–75), pp. 276–77.
3. P. Alexis, op. cit., Vol. II, pp. 24–25. Sister Paul-Émile and Hector Legros, *Le diocèse d'Ottawa (1847–1948)* (Ottawa: Le Droit, 1949), pp. 99, 108–10.
4. Sister Paul-Émile and Hector Legros, op. cit., p. 108.
5. Minutes (1872–1912), p. 18, meeting of 26 October 1879; letter from Father Champagne, 23 January 1880; archives of the parish of Saint-François-de-Sales, Gatineau. P. Alexis, op. cit., Vol. II, p. 226. Lucien Brault, *Histoire de la Pointe-Gatineau (1807–1947)* (Montreal: Éditions des Sourds-Muets, 1948), p. 109.
6. Letters of 3 January 1881 and 20 February 1882, Georges Bouillon file, archives of the archdiocese of Ottawa. *Buckingham: Son histoire, son patrimoine* (Buckingham, 1983), p. 30.
7. Excerpt, Chroniques de la maison mère, Vol. I, archives of the Sisters of Charity, Ottawa.
8. Minutes (1879–1906), archives of the parish of Sainte-Angélique, Papineauville. P. Alexis, op. cit., Vol. II, p. 286. *Album-souvenir du 75e anniversaire de la paroisse de Sainte-Angélique de Papineauville (1853–1928)* (Papineauville, 1928), p. 19. *1853–1978: Sainte-Angélique de Papineauville, 125 ans* (Papineauville, 1978), pp. 4, 21.
9. P. Alexis, op. cit., Vol. II, p. 213.
10. Luskville file, diocese of Hull, Inventaire des biens culturels, Ministère des Affaires culturelles, Province de Québec.
11. Letter of 6 July 1885, Saint-Jean-Baptiste file, I.6.65, archives of the archdiocese of Ottawa. Sister Paul-Émile and Hector Legros, op. cit., pp. 261–63.
12. Gaston Carrière, op. cit., Vol. VIII, pp. 65–66.
13. Accounts book, archives of the parish of St. Isidore, Kanata, South March. P. Alexis, op. cit., Vol. II, pp. 211–12.
14. P. Alexis, op. cit., Vol. II, p. 188. Courtney C. J. Bond, *The Ottawa Country: A Historical Guide to the National Capital Region* (Ottawa: Queen's Printer, 1968) (Published under the authority of the Department of Public Works), p. 181.
15. Letter from Father Champagne to Monsignor Duhamel, 8 November 1886; statement of accounts, 1887, p. 58; archives of the parish of Saint-François-de-Sales, Gatineau. P. Alexis, op. cit., Vol. II, p. 227. Lucien Brault, op. cit., p. 104.
16. Letter from Georges Bouillon to Monsignor Duhamel, 16 June 1888, Georges Bouillon file, archives of the archdiocese of Ottawa. P. Alexis, op. cit., Vol. II, p. 199. "Historique de la paroisse," undated press clipping (*Le Droit*?), file of Notre-Dame-de-Lourdes, Vanier (Eastview), archives of the archdiocese of Ottawa. Sister Paul-Émile and Hector Legros, op. cit., p. 328.
17. P. Alexis, op. cit., Vol. II, p. 403.
18. Letter of 3 May 1887 to the superior, correspondence of Monsignor Duhamel, archives of the archdiocese of Ottawa. Sister Paul-Émile and Hector Legros, op. cit., p. 717.
19. See chapter III on the history of the construction of the convent and the chapel.
20. Gaston Carrière, op. cit., Vol. VI, p. 195. *La Minerve*, 18 February 1889. P. Alexis, op. cit., Vol. II, p. 144.
21. Gaston Carrière, op. cit., Vol. VIII, p. 28. Letter from Father Augier, provincial, 12 July 1888, Mattawa file, archives of the province, Oblates of Mary Immaculate, Montreal.
22. P. Alexis, op. cit., Vol. II, p. 177.
23. *Le Soleil*, 11 November 1899, p. 11, and 23 March 1900, p. 8. Pierre-Georges Roy, *Dates Lévisiennes*, Vol. V, p. 37. Caron architectural collection, Archives nationales du Québec in Trois-Rivières.
24. Gaston Carrière, op. cit., Vol. VIII, p. 30.
25. Letters of 24 July 1878, 25 January 1893, 10 March 1893, 11 April 1893, 26 September 1902, Georges Bouillon file; letters from Joseph J.-B. Verret, 2 May 1901, 20 September 1902, correspondence of Monsignor Blais; report by architect L.-Z. Gauthier, 8 May 1901; series of plans by Georges Bouillon; archives of the diocese of Rimouski.
26. Letter of 28 April 1898 to Georges Bouillon, correspondence of Monsignor Blais, archives of the diocese of Rimouski. Accounts book, 1899; portfolio of interior decor plans by Georges Bouillon; archives of the parish of Sainte-Cécile-du-Bic. *Le Soleil*, 18 March 1899, p. 7. Joseph D. Michaud, *Le Bic: Les étapes d'une paroisse. Deuxième partie: Un siècle de vie paroissiale* (Quebec City: l'Action sociale, 1926), p. 100ff.
27. Antonin Plourde, *1872–1972: Saint-Jean-Baptiste d'Ottawa* (Ottawa, 1972), p. 31. Sister Paul-Émile and Hector Legros, op. cit., pp. 524–28.
28. Letters of 6 March 1899 and 12 February 1900, Georges Bouillon file; letter from Monsignor Blais to architect Joseph J.-B. Verret of 18 September 1899 and letter of 2 May 1901 from architect Verret to the bishop, correspondence of Monsignor Blais; series of plans signed G. Bouillon; archives of the diocese of Rimouski.
29. Letter to Georges Bouillon of 10 September 1898, correspondence of Monsignor Blais, archives of the diocese of Rimouski. Photograph of the convent shortly after construction (PA 23742), and the chapel inside the convent (PA 23799), National Photography Collection, National Archives of Canada, Ottawa.
30. Letter of 28 April 1898 to Georges Bouillon and letter of 4 June 1898 to the parish priest of Trois-Pistoles, correspondence of Monsignor Blais, archives of the diocese of Rimouski. Minutes (1868–1910), pp. 379, 385, meetings of 12 January 1901 and 16 March 1902; contract of 2 May 1902 with contractor J. H. Morin, with an estimate by J. Joseph Pierre Ouellet, signed before the notary Joseph-Mathias Michaud of Trois-Pistoles; seven sheets of plans by Georges Bouillon; archives of the parish of Notre-Dame, Trois-Pistoles.
31. Minutes (1872–1912), archives of the parish of Saint-François-de-Sales, Gatineau. Lucien Brault, op. cit., pp. 104–106.
32. Letter of 28 December 1902 from Georges Bouillon to Monsignor Blais, Georges Bouillon file, archives of the diocese of

Rimouski. D.-M.-A. Magnan, *Notice historique: Notre-Dame-de-Lourdes de Fall River, Mass.* (Quebec City, 1925), pp. 85–87.

33. Two sheets and three photographs of plans, Caron architectural collection, Archives nationales du Québec in Trois-Rivières. "The Cathedral of Nova Sancta Sophia," *Harper's Weekly*, New York, 1 November 1902, pp. 1585, 1616–19. Anson A. Gard, *The Hub and the Spokes, or the Capital and Its Environs* (Ottawa: Emerson Press, 1904), pp. 137–38.

34. Letter of 16 October 1903, Georges Bouillon file, archives of the diocese of Rimouski.

35. Minutes (1886–1920), meetings of 2 and 4 September 1904; payments to the architect, 1907 accounts; archives of the parish of Saint-Paul, Aylmer. Sister Paul-Émile and Hector Legros, op. cit., p. 148. Caron architectural collection, Archives nationales du Québec in Trois-Rivières.

36. Six sheets of plans for the "House of G. Bouillon," Georges Bouillon file, archives of the archdiocese of Ottawa.

37. Series of five plans: "Perspective and Proposed Plan for the Departmental Buildings, facing Major Hill Park, Dominion of Canada, Ottawa, Ont."; "Elevation of Proposed Plan for the Departmental Building, facing Sussex Street, Dominion of Canada, Ottawa, Ont."; "Elevation of Proposed Plan for the Departmental Building, facing Major Hill Park, Dominion of Canada, Ottawa, Ont."; "Perspective of Proposed Plan for the Justice Building, Dominion of Canada, Ottawa, Ont."; "Proposed Plan for the Justice Building, Dominion of Canada, Ottawa, Ont."; Caron architectural collection, Archives nationales du Québec in Trois-Rivières. *Construction*, October 1907, pp. 48–50. Robert G. Hill, entry on Georges Bouillon, *The Biographical Dictionary of Architects in Canada, 1800–1930* (forthcoming).

38. Floor plan of the museum planned for the Plains of Abraham in Quebec City, one sheet, Caron architectural collection, Archives nationales du Québec in Trois-Rivières.

39. Canon Georges Bouillon file, Gérard Morisset collection, Inventaire des biens culturels, Ministère des Affaires culturelles, Province de Québec.

40. Two sheets of plans, signed Canon Bouillon, designated as "Third plan proposed for the Church of St. Anthony in Manchester, New Hampshire"; Caron architectural collection, Archives nationales du Québec in Trois-Rivières.